SPORTS BABYLON

SPORTS BABYLON

SEX, DRUGS, AND OTHER DIRTY DEALINGS IN THE WORLD OF SPORTS

MARK SABLJAK & MARTIN H. GREENBERG

BELL PUBLISHING COMPANY
New York

To my brother John and sister Julie.
Grown up now, we're better friends than ever.
—Mark Sabljak

ACKNOWLEDGMENTS

Thanks to the members of the *Milwaukee Journal* sports staff, who offered suggestions for inclusions, particularly Pete Faust, Dick Pufall, Karl Svatek, Bob Wolf, and Bob Wolfley. Also, to Dana Burke. Finally, my appreciation to our editor, Cynthia Sternau, a good sport.

Published in 1988 by Bell Publishing Company, distributed by Crown Publishers, Inc., 225 Park Avenue South, New York, New York 10003.

Printed and bound in the United States of America

Library of Congress Cataloging-in-Publication Data

Sabljak, Mark.
  Sports Babylon : sex, drugs, and other dirty dealings in the world of sports / by Mark Sabljak and Martin H. Greenberg.
  1. Sports—United States—Corrupt practices. 2. Sports—United States—Miscellanea. I. Greenberg, Martin Harry. II. Title.
GV718.2.U6S23   1988
796′.0973—dc19   88–5982
                                                                            CIP

ISBN 0–517–66717–7
h g f e d c b
First Edition

Contents

Introduction

Every sport has its record book filled with the accomplishments of teams, players, and coaches. Their heights, weights, home towns, record-setting games, seasons, and careers are recorded there for posterity. The whole story is written in those lists and tables. Or is it really?

The "official" histories of many sports completely and conveniently skip over anything that could be termed "negative." How many commissioners have stood before a microphone and uttered the phrases "bad for baseball," or "bad for football"? Negative incidents are met with official dismay, then swept under the rug, filed forever in the chapter that never seems to make the "official" book.

This book is an "unofficial" history of the world of sports. Athletes don't always have good characters, and not everyone maintains grace and good manners under stress and humiliation. The figures in our history are zany, tragic, and sometimes just plain pathetic. They lie, laugh, cheat, dream, steal, win, and—sometimes—they die. Don't look for reasons, however. No one can explain why. Even the greatest sports superstars are still human.

Sports Babylon tells the stories of assorted abusers, blunderers, braggarts, brats, crack-ups, criminals, fighters, flakes, and philanderers, whose escapades haven't always made stellar sports history. These all-too-human portraits prove that even the best can sometimes do the worst. It's everyone for himself in the dog-eat-dog world of competitive sports, and honor is often left on the bench.

As with any history, official or unofficial, life continues and events must occur after the presses have rolled. We cannot claim that this "unofficial" history is complete, for then there would be no more sports world. But we do believe that you'll find a fascinating gallery of sports figures and human frailties worthy of reading and passing on to the next generation.

ABUSE

LEN BIAS

DWIGHT GOODEN

GARY McLAIN

ART SCHLICHTER

JACK LAMBERT

THE PITTSBURGH ELEVEN

VIDA BLUE

Why is it that we expect so much more from athletes than we do from any other human beings? Is it the high pedestal on which we've placed sports heroes? When athletes fall prey to drugs, alcohol, or even gambling, they seem to fall farther and land harder than anyone else.

LEN BIAS

THE BOSTON CELTICS retired Jersey No. 30 in June 1986. But the player to whom the jersey belonged had never scored a point for the Celtics and had never even played for the team.

Len Bias's story may be one of the most tragic in sports history. Bias died of a heart attack caused by cocaine just a day after he was chosen by the Celtics for the number-two spot in the entire National Basketball Association draft. His death jolted the already shell-shocked sports world and the entire United States as well.

According to testimony given at the trial of Brian Tribble, Bias's friend who was charged with (but later acquitted of) supplying the cocaine he used, Bias's death scene began at 2:30 in the morning when the basketball star woke teammate Terry Long and asked him to help celebrate his new contract with the Celtics.

Long said he left his room for a moment, and when he returned, Bias and Tribble were standing next to a large quantity of cocaine— Long demonstrated the amount by pouring about a half a cup of coffee creamer onto a mirror. He said that the party was interrupted when another Maryland player, Jeff Baxter, entered the room and the drugs were put away. After Baxter left, at about 4:30, the cocaine snorting continued, and around 6:30, Bias appeared "messed up." "After we saw he couldn't make it to the bathroom on his own, we told him to recline on the bed," said Long.

Bias then went into convulsions and paramedics were called. An autopsy showed traces of cocaine in his blood. It was said to have caused a spasm that, in turn, apparently caused blood clots to form in an artery. The blocked artery led to a lethal heart attack.

Bias's death also ended the Maryland career of Lefty Driesell, who was considered one of the top coaches in the college game. In the days afterward, Driesell said that he "didn't know what happened" and that for Bias to use drugs would have been "completely out of character."

It was Driesell who spoke of Bias's accomplishments at Maryland in a memorial service: a school record of 2,149 points scored and selection for the All-American team. Driesell went on to say, "But I want to talk about Leonard as a man. Leonard was a kind person, one who would say, 'Thank you' if you did something for him. He was intelligent, loving, and he cared for his fellow human beings."

Driesell later admitted he knew within hours that Bias's death was caused by drugs and that he met with players Terry Long and David Gregg in the basement of his home before noon on the morning Bias died. Gregg also testified later that after Bias collapsed, he (Gregg) put the remains of a large mound of cocaine in a plastic bag and gave it to Tribble. When asked why he did it, Gregg said, "To protect the image of Len Bias. I didn't want anybody to know what he was doing."

After the paramedics arrived, they asked everyone in the room if Bias took drugs. The answer was no. Gregg said that he had used cocaine eight to ten times before the morning Bias died, half the time with Bias, and that on three occasions, Bias had been the supplier of the drug.

Bias's death was immediately seized upon by lawmakers, who moved to stiffen penalties for drug suppliers involved in fatal overdose cases. Bias's mother, Lonise, also took her son's message to the public, returning to College Park, Maryland, half a year later to speak to students. "You have got to love yourself first and not use drugs," she told several hundred University of Maryland students. "You can make it. If I can stand here today, there's nothing you can't do. Believe me, you can make it.

"When was the best time to take Lenny? It's when everyone's eyes are on him, when you have the number-two player on the number-one team and everyone's screaming, 'Lenny, Lenny, Lenny.' And then, swoosh, he's snatched away. By that time, God has everyone's attention. If it were not for the death of Len Bias, I would be at home with my four children—one of them playing for the Celtics, or wherever—and I would not know the state of the country today, and it is pitiful."

Bobby Knight, the Indiana University basketball coach, also pointed to Bias's death as an example, but with less pity in his voice. "In the last ten years, the two best college basketball players I've seen are Bias and Michael Jordan," Knight told a basketball camp. "But I don't feel sorry for Len Bias. Len Bias had his own mind and his own body to take care of, and he didn't do it. If some of you are popping pills or smoking dope, those are bad shots you are taking. Len Bias was better than anybody in this room . . . but he's dead. He's not sick, he's not hurt, he's dead. He just wasn't strong enough to take care of himself. He wanted to be one of the boys. He wanted to be cool. Well, he was so cool, he's cold. He's as cold as heck."

DWIGHT GOODEN

ON APRIL FOOL'S DAY of 1986, Dwight Gooden was ordered to undergo drug treatment. It was no joke. Dwight Gooden was the youngest pitcher ever to win the Cy Young Award, baseball's youngest millionaire, star pitcher for the World Series champion New York Mets, and the hero of millions of youths, particularly black youngsters.

Gooden, twenty-three, had days earlier taken one of a series of voluntary drug tests, and flunked. He was confronted by team officials and told he would either have to begin a drug treatment program or be suspended by baseball commissioner Peter Ueberroth. Gooden's first reaction, according to Mets' general manager Frank Cashen, was to say, "I don't know how this could be." Then, Cashen said, he grew silent. "He was kind of decimated. He was very quiet." Gooden's attorney, Charles Ehrlich, said, "We're talking about cocaine." Gooden's teammates were, of course, shocked. Darryl Strawberry said, "I know him closer than anyone on this ball club. And I cannot believe he had any problem."

In retrospect, it should have been obvious, because the pitcher was involved in a clear trail of incidents. After a spectacular 1985 season, in which he had a 24–4 record, 1.53 ERA, 268 strikeouts, and won the Cy Young Award, Gooden dropped to a 17–6 record in 1986, with a 2.84 ERA, and 200 strikeouts. He also failed to win a game throughout the playoffs and the World Series.

Off the field, it was even worse. Before the 1986 season, he failed to tell the Mets he had suffered a sprained ankle and then refused to have his ankle examined by the team. During spring training in 1986, Gooden had a mysterious auto accident that caused him to miss a game, and he was later involved in a dispute at a car rental counter in New York.

He missed the Mets' World Series parade with what he called a "stomach ache," but later it was found he had had a fight with his fiancée, and the two eventually canceled their wedding plans. At the same time, Gooden's father acknowledged that his son had fathered a child out of wedlock with another woman.

In January of 1987 his former fiancée, Carlene Pearson, was arrested at La Guardia Airport with a handgun in her purse as she was going to meet Gooden on an incoming plane.

The most famous incident was Gooden's scuffle with Tampa police after a car he was riding in was stopped for a minor traffic violation. Gooden later pleaded no contest to charges of battery on a police officer and resisting arrest with violence, and was placed on three-years probation.

Why did Gooden agree to be tested for drug use? Cashen said, "When he signed his contract in January, he asked to be tested. He was tired of hearing all those allegations. We agreed to test one time in spring training. Why would he agree to be tested when he knew he had taken drugs? I don't know. A lot of us think we can handle anything. Some people take four drinks, and they're still certain they can pass the sobriety test. We all think we're immortal." Mets' manager Davey Johnson said, "The thought I can't get rid of is that he had to want to get caught. I can't understand it."

Gooden successfully completed a drug rehabilitation program, in which it was determined he was an occasional cocaine user, not an addict. He returned to pitch in the 1987 season, helping the Mets stay in their division race to the very end. He also apparently steered clear of any further drug use and finished with a 15–7 record, a 3.21 ERA, and 148 strikeouts.

His brush with drugs was not without its consequences, however. Advertisers who were used to hiring athletes for endorsements began to look twice at the idea. And more than one hero-worshipping youngster was sent searching in another direction for an untarnished idol.

GARY McLAIN

NOT TOO MANY basketball players get to make a trip to the final four of the NCAA tournament. Even fewer also visit the White House. There is probably only one who did both while high on drugs. This shocking revelation was made in March of 1987 by Gary McLain, a former basketball player at Villanova, in an article in *Sports Illustrated*.

McLain, a starter on the team, said he was high on cocaine during Villanova's semifinal game against Memphis State in the 1985 NCAA tournament. He had nine points and two assists in the game, and Villanova then went on to upset Georgetown to win the national title, a game in which McLain had eight points and two assists.

Writing about his visit to the White House, McLain said, "I was standing in the Rose Garden wired on cocaine." About President Ronald Reagan, he added, "I was standing a couple of feet behind him, looking in his hair, thinking, this guy has more dandruff than your average man. [I was] thinking thoughts like, 'I could push him in the head, just a little tap, and make news across the world.' "

Even to an already jaded sports world, McLain's confession— printed in a cover story of *Sports Illustrated*—was met with shock. McLain's coach at Villanova, the well-respected Rollie Massimino, took it the hardest. Massimino said it was the "most devastating thing that has happened to me in thirty years of coaching. I am crushed, I really, really am." An immediate inquiry conducted by the school exonerated Massimino of any knowledge of the situation.

McLain, meanwhile, said he had received drug treatment in 1986 after losing a job on Wall Street. McLain also revealed that he had used a quarter gram of "blow" before the NCAA semifinal in the bathroom of a room in the Ramada Inn, about three miles from the game's site, the Rupp Arena in Lexington. Because he was so quiet in the locker room before the game, he said that teammates, who later swore they knew nothing of his drug use, asked him, "You all right? You all right?" He responded, "Yeah, I'm with it." But, he said, he had gotten it in his head that "if we lost it didn't matter. I just wanted the season to be over."

In 1987 McLain joined the list of ex-athletes speaking about the dangers of drug abuse.

ART SCHLICHTER

PRO FOOTBALL scouts liked what they saw in quarterback Art Schlichter. He had size, he had "quick feet," and he was mobile. Ohio State University coeds also rated him highly. "Art is just a big, handsome farm boy who has everything," one said.

Well, he *had* almost everything. For a guy with a college career that included leading his team to the Rose Bowl and a first-round spot in the NFL college draft in 1982, Schlichter (pronounced SHLEE-ster) had a very brief and very dismal pro career. It wasn't an injury that cut short a promising career, however; it was gambling.

Schlichter blew an estimated $1,609,000 on gambling during his final years at Ohio State and his first year with the Baltimore Colts. Reports of Schlichter's involvement with gambling caught the football world by surprise. Those reports said Schlichter decided to help FBI agents build a case against four Baltimore-area men who were subsequently arrested.

According to the reports, Schlichter began cooperating in the investigation after bookmakers reportedly pushed him for payment and threatened to tell the Colts about his gambling. The NFL, by now accustomed to dealing with drug problems, reacted with lightning speed and suspended Schlichter indefinitely while conducting its own investigation.

Schlichter began treatment for compulsive gambling, and in an interview given shortly after the incident, said, "I have not only been a compulsive gambler for too long, it made me a compulsive liar. I've been living a life with lies compounding lies. Thank God this part of it is in the open now. . . ."

Like many compulsive gamblers, Schlichter grew up in an atmosphere that condoned gambling. There were race tracks near the Ohio farm where he was raised, and his mother and other relatives owned race horses. But Schlichter kept his gambling secret even from his family. In hindsight, however, those close to him feel his secret life began to show during his first year in the pros, when, despite his great promise, he was used only sparingly. Apparently, Schlichter's mind was on where his next bet would come from and not on learning the team's plays.

After his reinstatement in June of 1984, Schlichter played in nine games in the 1984 season and appeared to have turned himself around when the Colts, now in Indianapolis, moved him to the starting position for the first game of the regular 1985 season. After the game, however, he never played another down, and in October the Colts released him. Despite his athletic attributes, the team said he lacked the arm power to throw passes the way the Colts wanted him to. Schlichter hooked up with the Buffalo Bills before the 1986 season, but he was cut during the exhibition season.

In January of 1987 he was arrested for gambling when it was disclosed he had bet $232,000 during a seventy-day period in the fall of 1986. He was eventually fined eighty-four dollars and placed on six-months probation.

JACK LAMBERT

The campaign against drug abuse, particularly in sports, has led to a widely used slogan: "Just Say No." But Jack Lambert, the tough-guy linebacker for the Pittsburgh Steelers, had a better idea. Lambert told a group of kids that if you're approached by someone who offers to sell you drugs, "Just punch them in the nose."

THE PITTSBURGH ELEVEN

These eleven players were fined by baseball commissioner Peter Ueberroth as a result of the Pittsburgh cocaine trial in September of 1985:

JOAQUIN ANDUJAR
DALE BERRA
ENOS CABELL
KEITH HERNANDEZ
AL HOLLAND
LEE LACY
JEFFREY LEONARD
DAVE PARKER
LONNIE SMITH
LARY SORENSEN
CLAUDELL WASHINGTON

VIDA BLUE

Vida Blue won a Cy Young Award with the Oakland As in 1971. But his career ended in 1987, when he suddenly announced his retirement. Blue took part in a drug rehabilitation program late in 1986 but refused to discuss drugs or the program. He left behind these words: "I never was into drugs. They were just positive urine tests. I'll get into all that at the proper time."

Len Bias

Dwight Gooden in action against the Chicago Cubs (AP/Wide World Photos)

Former Villanova basketball player Gary McLain discusses his
drug use on the "Today Show." (AP/Wide World Photos)

Art Schlichter

Jack Lambert—would you try to sell drugs to this man?

Jack Lambert on the field

Joaquin Andujar

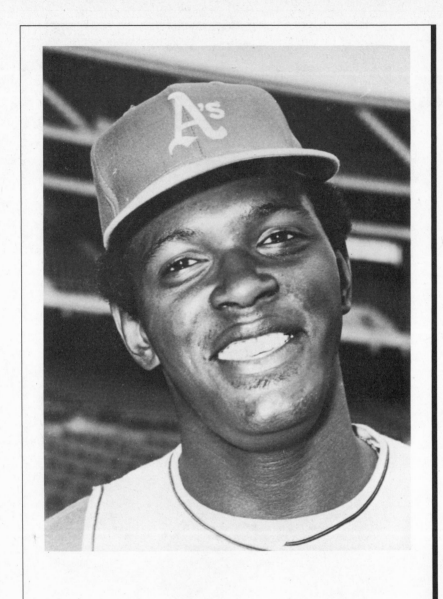

Vida Blue

BLUNDERS

FRED BROWN

GARO YEPREMIAN

CRAIG STADLER

HART, ROBINSON, AND TAYLOR

WILLIE SHOEMAKER

MARY BACON

MITCH GREEN

The history of sports has been littered with mistakes and miscues. Some were hilarious, with little effect on the final score, while others were costly in both defeats and dollars.

FRED BROWN

ARE THERE a few seconds in your life you'd like to live over again? Be happy you're not Fred Brown, whose bad seconds occurred on national television. On the night of March 30, 1982—in front of a live crowd of 62,000 and a national television audience in the millions—Brown made a mistake that was thereafter known as "the phantom pass."

Brown's Georgetown squad was up against North Carolina in the NCAA basketball tournament championship final at the Louisiana Superdome. North Carolina was in the lead, 63–62, on a sixteen-foot jump shot by superstar Michael Jordan. But Georgetown had the ball and fifteen seconds remained, plenty of time to score and win the game and the NCAA title.

Georgetown inbounded the ball quickly, hoping to catch North Carolina off guard. Sure enough, as Brown dribbled the ball upcourt, North Carolina's James Worthy trailed in the backcourt. A North Carolina player stepped up to challenge Brown, who—out of the corner of his eye, so he said—thought he saw a teammate open alongside. He passed the ball—to North Carolina's Worthy.

"I saw [Eric] Floyd cut to the right side, and I thought he was open, so I picked up my dribble to pass it, but then nobody was free, so I thought I'd throw it to Eric Smith on the other side," Brown explained. "I was surprised," said Worthy. "It was right in my chest. I saw him [Brown] pick up the ball at the top of the key. He was going to throw to someone on the wings. I thought he'd try to lob it over me or throw it away from me."

Worthy tried to dribble the remaining seconds off the clock but was fouled by Smith with two seconds left. He missed both free throws, but a desperation shot at the buzzer by Georgetown's Floyd didn't come close. The snafu gave Dean Smith, North Carolina's respected coach, his first NCAA title.

While North Carolina celebrated with hugs and rides on the shoulder, there were tears of disappointment on the Georgetown bench. But Coach John Thompson would have none of it. He went up to each of his fourteen players and said something personal. What did he say to Brown? "I told Freddie that he had won more games for us than he had lost. I told him not to worry, it was one of those human errors."

GARO YEPREMIAN

THE SUPER BOWL is not a good place to learn a new position, especially if the position is quarterback. When Garo Yepremian, a 5-foot 8-inch placekicker, attempted to throw a touchdown pass in Super Bowl VII, the pass did end up as a touchdown—but not for Yepremian's Miami Dolphins. What had been a comfortable time for Dolphin fans to that point, suddenly turned tense.

Yepremian might have locked up Miami's first Super Bowl title and a 17–0 season when he lined up to attempt a forty-two-yard field goal with two and a half minutes remaining. The Dolphins led the Washington Redskins, 14–0, and a successful field goal would have made it 17–0, forcing the Redskins to score three times even to tie the game. But when the ball left Yepremian's foot, it traveled only a few yards before being blocked by Washington's Bill Brundige. "I think it was low," Miami coach Don Shula said.

The ball bounced once on the ground, and Yepremian picked it up. "He should have fallen on it," Shula said later. Yepremian cocked his arm to throw the ball, but the ball squirted into the air. Then the Cypriot native who once voiced his intention to "keek a touchdown," tried his hand at volleyball and attempted to bat the ball out of bounds. "He should have fallen on it," Shula said again, more sternly. Yepremian batted the ball to Washington's Mike Bass, who ran for forty-nine yards and scored the Redskins' only touchdown.

With the extra point conversion the Redskins were back in the ball game. But Washington decided not to try an onside kick, and Miami did a good job of holding on to the ball. After the punt, the Redskins' best offensive chance in the final seconds ended with quarterback Bill Kilmer flat on his back, six yards behind the line of scrimmage, with two Dolphin defensive players draped over him.

After the game Yepremian was questioned about the play. One of his answers would undoubtedly have met with the approval of his coach. "I guess I should have fallen on it," Yepremian said. Adding more insight, he said, "I guess I made a mistake." He also admitted that the final minutes of the game were horrific. "I never prayed so much," he said. "God came through for me." Of his decision to throw the ball, Yepremian said that he "saw some white jerseys downfield. . . . I thought I was doing something good, something to help the team. Instead it was almost a tragedy. I almost caused a disaster."

Yepremian's teammate, Earl Morrall, said that the snap from center Howard Kindig was low and that "Garo hit it good, but they broke through to block it." In the other locker room, Bass said, "I heard the thump when the ball was blocked. And it's my job to get the ball when it's blocked. Then I saw Garo with the ball and I knew from our years in Detroit that he wasn't going to run with it. He picked up the ball and it slipped out of his hand when he tried to throw it. When he tried to get it back, he kind of batted it into the air. That's when I got it."

With the trophy safely tucked away, Miami quarterback Bob Griese was able to laugh about the situation. "I've got to work with Garo," he said. Yepremian, however, wasn't all that sure it was a laughing matter. "Wouldn't it have been terrible after we won sixteen games in a row if we had lost because of that play?"

CRAIG STADLER

THE MOST expensive towel in history is probably not in a hotel or a museum; it's in Craig Stadler's golf bag. Stadler pulled out the towel and put it on the wet ground to keep his knees dry as he knelt to make a shot during the Professional Golfers Association tour event in San Diego in February of 1987. He made the shot during the third round, put the towel away, and played on.

But Stadler's game had been recorded, and when it was shown on television the next day, it elicited several phone calls to the tournament office from viewers who were wondering about the towel. Sure enough, the use of a towel was illegal and against PGA rules—rule 13-3½—which says a golfer cannot "build" a stance.

Stadler could have taken a two-stroke penalty at the time and continued to play, had he realized the violation. He didn't know this, however, and at the end of the tournament he signed his scorecard, thinking he had finished in a three-way tie for second place—worth $37,333.33. Moments later he learned he was disqualified and would receive no prize money after all.

A member of the PGA rules staff explained, "The TV network had some clips from yesterday that they showed today. Several people called our office in the press room and asked, 'Is this legal?' It is not. Stadler signed his scorecard for lower than he should have. He was disqualified. The rule is new this year. It was drafted in April of 1986. I'm sure he didn't realize he was violating the rule, but it's his responsibility to know the rules."

29

If that wasn't enough for one golfer in one season, Stadler's woes continued later in the tour. In the July British Open, held in Muirfield, Scotland, he took a two-shot penalty when he removed a ball from a wet area in the gallery on the fifth hole. In the United States, he would have been allowed to take a drop from the spot, and that is exactly what he did.

Spectators again reported the incident, which was not legal according to British Open rules. But this time Stadler still had time to rectify the error, and he gave himself a two-shot penalty on the hole. "At least, this time, I'm still playing," he said. "I'm still in the tournament." Stadler added, "Some day, I'm going to learn the rules. I'm going to take a month off and read the rules and the decisions on the rules."

HART, ROBINSON, AND TAYLOR

"I HAVE seen lots of guys lose gold medals—but never sitting in front of a TV set watching themselves do it." With those words, columnist Jim Murray of the *Los Angeles Times* began one of the most tragic stories in Olympic history. It was the story of three U.S. sprinters—Eddie Hart, Reynaud Robinson, and Robert Taylor—who went to the 1972 Summer Olympics in Munich, West Germany, with a chance of sweeping the top three places in the 100-meter event.

Robinson was coholder of the world record in the 100 with a time of 9.9 seconds, and Hart had been called "the best runner in the world" by his coach that year. Either could have won the gold medal in the 100-meter event at the Olympics.

But at the time they were supposed to line up for the quarterfinal qualifying heat, they were watching the competition on television in a bungalow in the nearby Olympic village. Robinson turned to his fellow television viewers and asked, "Is that on tape or something?" It wasn't. It was live. Realizing they were supposed to be at the track, the three men sprinted to a car and raced to the stadium. Though they arrived before the race began, there wasn't enough time for them to warm up properly; Taylor finished second, Robinson and Hart last.

Why didn't the athletes get to the stadium on time? Their coach, Stan Wright, took full blame, saying he misread the schedule. "It was my fault, my fault," he told reporters on the scene. "I'll talk to you later."

Hart and Robinson did not disagree with their coach. Robinson told the press, "I don't care, the man is the coach. He can say he's sorry. What about three years, what about torn ligaments, pulled muscles, a broken leg? What about all those [bleep] meets, all that bullsmoke in Tuskegee and Alabama State? Shee! This is the big one. This is what it's all about. And we sit there looking at pictures. He told us seven o'clock. We were going over to warm up. The man's a coach. He supposed to get his sprinters on the blocks. What else he got more important to do?"

Sportscaster Howard Cosell, in his best form, called the incident "an American tragedy!" Teammates admitted they had trouble looking Robinson and Hart in the eye during the rest of the games, and another newspaper writer said Wright's blunder had earned him a spot in history along with wrong-way Riegels and baseball's Fred Merkle.

Four years later, Hart had retired and Robinson was trying to make the United States Olympic team again. Robinson declined to talk about his 1972 experience again, saying, "It's not a touchy subject, but I'm just tired of talking and hearing about it. I don't have anything else to say about it. I want to forget about it. Everything is the same as before; if anything, it made me get into the sport more. I learned more about track and field, not just as a competitor, but about teaching and learning the sport."

Robinson failed to make the team.

WILLIE SHOEMAKER

WILLIE SHOEMAKER may be the greatest jockey of all time, but in 1957, in horse racing's premier event, the Kentucky Derby, he made one of the sport's biggest mistakes.

Shoe, as he is known, began his career in 1949, and by the time of the 1957 Derby at Churchill Downs, he had already achieved a great degree of success. And it appeared that he would add another feather to his cap, when, atop Gallant Man, he headed toward the finish line among the leaders. But at the sixteenth pole, with a green starter's stand alongside, he rose momentarily from his saddle. Gallant Man sensed the move, eased up, and was beaten by a nose at the wire by Iron Liege. To make matters worse, Shoemaker was suspended for fifteen days by Churchill Downs' stewards for "gross carelessness' in misjudging the point of finish of the race.

Two years later, Shoemaker vindicated himself by riding Tomy Lee to a close victory in the eighty-fifth Kentucky Derby. Famed columnist Red Smith wrote on that occasion, describing the place on the track where Shoemaker had stood up, "Willie knows that spot. It was here he made the most scarifying mistake of his life two years ago. Then, thinking he was home with Gallant Man, he had eased his mount just long enough to let Iron Liege rush by for the money. Where he quit riding that day, he started riding Saturday."

Nineteen years later, when Shoemaker wrote his own story, he intimated that he hadn't made a mistake, but had merely conceded the race because he knew he was going to lose. "I don't think I ever made the lead in that Derby," Shoemaker wrote. ". . . I thought the race was over and I'd lost when I stood up. Eventually, the winning margin was a nose, which was as close as I got to Iron Liege. . . . The truth is I really don't know whether my mistake made him lose the race or not."

Twenty-nine years after the Derby mistake, on the occasion of his fourth Derby victory, in 1986, Shoemaker was still being reminded of his mistake by journalists. He was fifty-four, and the greatest career in horse racing—albeit one with a giant error—was still going strong.

World's highest-paid athletes

1991 rank	1990 rank	Athlete	Sport	Salary or winnings	Other income ($ million)	Total
1	10	Evander Holyfield	Boxing	$60.0	$0.5	$60.5
2	1	Mike Tyson	Boxing	30	1.5	31.5
3	8	Michael Jordan	Basketball	2.8	13.2	16.0
4	NR	George Foreman	Boxing	14.0	0.5	14.5
5	4	Ayrton Senna	Auto racing	12.0	1.0	13.0
6	5	Alain Prost	Auto racing	10.0	1.0	11.0
7	NR	Razor Ruddock	Boxing	10.0	0.2	10.2
8	9	Arnold Palmer	Golf	0.3	9.0	9.3
9	12	Nigel Mansell	Auto racing	8.0	1.0	9.0
10	6	Jack Nicklaus	Golf	0.5	8.0	8.5
11	NR	Larry Bird	Basketball	7.4	0.5	7.9
12	NR	Monica Seles	Tennis	1.6	6.0	7.6
13	25	Joe Montana	Football	3.5	4.0	7.5
14	17	Stefan Edberg	Tennis	1.4	6.0	7.4
14	7	Greg Norman	Golf	0.4	7.0	7.4
16	13	Steffi Graf	Tennis	1.3	6.0	7.3
16	16	Andre Agassi	Tennis	0.8	6.5	7.3
18	11	Boris Becker	Tennis	1.2	6.0	7.2
19	15	Wayne Gretzky	Hockey	3.0	4.0	7.0
19	28	Gerhard Berger	Auto racing	6.0	1.0	7.0
21	NR	Jean Alesi	Auto racing	6.0	0.5	6.5
22	22	Gabriela Sabatini	Tennis	1.3	5.0	6.3
23	23	Magic Johnson	Basketball	2.5	3.0	5.5
24	NR	David Robinson	Basketball	2.4	3.0	5.4
24	NR	Nick Faldo	Golf	0.4	5.0	5.4
26	NR	Jennifer Capriati	Tennis	0.6	4.5	5.1
27	NR	Raghib Ismail	Football	4.5	0.5	5.0
27	26	Patrick Ewing	Basketball	4.0	1.0	5.0
29	NR	John Williams	Basketball	4.8	0.1	4.9
30	18	Ivan Lendl	Tennis	0.8	4.0	4.8
31	21	Bo Jackson	Baseball/football	2.0	2.5	4.5
32	NR	Pete Sampras	Tennis	0.4	4.0	4.4
33	NR	Hakeem Olajuwon	Basketball	3.8	0.5	4.3
33	NR	Darryl Strawberry	Baseball	3.8	0.5	4.3
33	27	Greg LeMond	Cycling	1.8	2.5	4.3
36	30	Will Clark	Baseball	3.8	0.4	4.2
36	NR	Nelson Piquet	Auto racing	4.0	0.2	4.2
38	NR	Kevin Mitchell	Baseball	3.8	0.3	4.1
39	29	Curtis Strange	Golf	0.5	3.5	4.0
40	NR	Joe Carter	Baseball	3.7	0.2	3.9

8-5-91

Source: Forbes

BASEBALL/AMERICAN

Coverage, 1, 4, 6C

Toronto 2, Boston 1	Milwaukee 3, Texas 2
Kansas City 2, Cleveland 0	Seattle 5, California 2 (12 inn.)
Detroit 8, New York 7 (10 inn.)	Minnesota 6, Oakland 2
Chicago 1, Baltimore 0	

NATIONAL

Coverage, 1, 5, 6C

Phila. 3, Montreal 2 (10 inn.)	Houston 2, L.A. 1 (10 inn.)
Atlanta 9, San Diego 7	Chicago 8, New York 3
Pittsburgh 2, St. Louis 1	Cincinnati 6, San Francisco 5

NFL EXHIBITION

Coverage, 1 7C

Pittsburgh 16, Washington 7

SPORTS HOT LINE: 1-900-933-3000

Call 24 hours a day for sports scores, horse racing results
and lottery numbers. Press 3 for access to this information.
See complete instructions, page 4D.
Cost: 95¢ a minute

BRAGGING RIGHTS: Florida's big three —
Florida State, Miami and Florida — might claim some
attention this year. All three are ranked in most preseason
football polls and, in the final two weeks of the season, the
Seminoles play Miami, then Florida. The winner could
walk away with the No. 1 national ranking.

SKINNED: Neil O'Donnell's 34-yard touchdown pass
and Gary Anderson's 54-yard field goal keyed a fourth-
quarter surge that gave the Pittsburgh Steelers a 16-7
victory against the Washington Redskins Sunday night in
their NFL exhibition opener. *(NFL report, 7C)*

MAKING BASKETS: Chris Webber of Birming-
ham (Mich.) Detroit Country Day, USA TODAY's 1991 high
school boys basketball player of the year, had 38 points to
lead Detroit Superfriends to a 95-75 win against Richmond
(Va.) Metro for the AAU Junior
Olympic title. *(Story, 10C)*

REFUELS: Joe Amato became the fifth Top Fuel driver

HAVANA — Brazil, which
knows how to play basketball
and celebrate, did both in upsetting the U.S. women's team
87-84 Sunday at the Pan American Games.

The USA, defending Olym-
pic and world champions who
last lost in a major tournament
at the 1982 World Champion-
ships, had a 42-game winning
streak stopped. Maria "Paula"
da Silva, who scored 22 points,
led the celebration with a dou-
ble cartwheel at midcourt.

"We beat the Olympic and
world champions, how do you
think I feel?" said Brazil coach
Maria Cardoso, who paid her

Pirate

Stealing

MARY BACON

Not all athletes make their mistakes on the field or during competition. Mary Bacon's big mistake happened on a soapbox.

Bacon was a female jockey who seemed to have the world by the tail in the mid-1970s. She brought femininity, beauty, and more than a bit of sex to a male-dominated sport. A winner on horses at major tracks, she posed nude in *Playboy* and became a national celebrity.

At the apparent peak of her success, she was filmed at a Ku Klux Klan rally on April 4, 1975, in Walker, Louisiana, where she told the audience, "We are not just a bunch of illiterate Southern nigger killers. We are good, white, Christian people, hard-working people working for a white America. When one of your wives or one of your sisters gets raped by a nigger, maybe you'll get smart and join the Klan."

It didn't take long for Bacon's speech to make its way across the country—and it took a much shorter time for her to lose a lucrative television commercial contract for Dutch Masters cigars and an endorsement deal with Revlon.

Good mounts began disappearing. And so eventually did Bacon, the victim of her runaway mouth.

MITCH GREEN

Professional boxers are not always at their best behind the wheel of a car. Heavyweight Mitch Green was pulled over by police in New York City in August of 1987 because he had a small television set on his dashboard. The police found several other interesting items in Green's car. The finds included pills, a bag of "angel dust," and a driving record that said Green, thirty years old, had had his license suspended fifty-four times. Green was charged with criminal possession of a controlled substance and driving without a valid license.

Garo Yepremian

Bob Griese

Craig Stadler flips his club in disgust after losing his lead during the 1985 Bob Hope Classic at Indian Wells. (AP/Wide World Photos)

Craig Stadler—the Walrus in happier times (AP/Wide World Photos)

Mary Bacon, splattered with mud after a race at the Big A
(AP/Wide World Photos)

BRAGGARTS

MUHAMMAD ALI

BRIAN BOSWORTH

JOE NAMATH

RIGGS VERSUS KING

LARRY HOLMES

They say that at the top of any sport, mental advantages give one player the edge over another. Confidence in one's ability to succeed is such an attribute. But you can also overdo it. These athletes did, regularly.

MUHAMMAD ALI

WHICH MUHAMMAD ALI do you remember? Is it Cassius Clay, the eighteen-year-old Olympic medal winner? Or is it Muhammad Ali, the boxing exile, who returned to win the world championship three times and became one of the most recognized faces in the world? Do you recall Ali, pitifully fat in his final years as a boxer, or Ali mumbling through interviews due to a bout with Parkinson's disease? Most would say they remember Ali the champion—mouth roaring and fists blazing—the Ali who proclaimed, "I am the greatest," and went on to become just that.

Just as important as a record of Ali's big fights is a list of some of his more outrageous statements.

—Why he refused induction into the army: "I ain't got no quarrel with them Viet Cong."

—To Howard Cosell, who had just said, "You're a bright boy, Muhammad": "You're not as dumb as you look."

—To reporters: "You writers seem fascinated to see black fighters go broke. You write that it's terrible that poor Joe Louis is broke. Well, Rolls-Royce is broke. The Penn Central is broke. The Catholic schools is broke."

—To reporters before a fight with George Foreman: "I want you guys to remember one thing: Black guys scare white guys a lot more than black guys scare black guys."

Ali knew his chattering and predictions infuriated his opponents and incited the crowds against him. To a question shouted at him—"How does it feel to be booed, loudmouth?"—he replied, "It's a good feeling to enter the ring with thousands of people booing you. Especially when you know you can deliver what you predict."

Where did Ali's vocal style come from? He says he picked it up from an opponent in the Olympic trials, an enemy who talked to him during the entire bout. Ali (then Cassius Clay) won and went on to take the Olympic gold medal in the light heavyweight class in 1960.

Ali, who admitted he admired the boastful style of wrestler Gorgeous George, turned pro in 1960, and won the heavyweight title in 1964 against Sonny Liston, a fight preceded by a press conference in which Ali appeared hysterical, lunged at Liston, and called his opponent a "chump" and an "ugly old bear." Shortly afterward Ali announced his membership in the Nation of Islam and then refused to fight in Vietnam because of his religious beliefs. Fight authorities stripped Ali of his title and boxing license, a federal court found him guilty of violating the Selective Service Act, and Ali went into professional exile from 1967 to 1970.

He returned to professional boxing when the Supreme Court reversed his conviction and finally won the title again in 1974 against George Foreman in Zaire, a fight Ali dubbed, "the rumble in the jungle." Ali lost the heavyweight title to a youthful Leon Spinks in 1978. But he recaptured the title against Spinks in New Orleans, and announced his retirement in 1979. He came back to fight for the vacant heavyweight title in 1980 but lost on a TKO to Larry Holmes. Ali fought his final bout against unheralded Trevor Berbick in 1981, losing a ten-round decision.

Ali is estimated to have won $69 million for sixty-one fights. His three marriages, however, cost him mightily. Even more drastic a toll was the effect of twenty-one years of boxing. In 1983 *Sports Illustrated* reported that Ali was suffering from physical abnormalities caused by boxing. During his interviews Ali's once loud oratory became a soft mumble. And in 1987 doctors admitted Ali was suffering from Parkinson's disease, caused by injuries to the brain sustained during his career.

Once seemingly unflappable, Ali said he would probably have to undergo surgery some day. "I know I'm sick and I know it's getting worse," he said. "I can't talk when I want to. Can't talk as fast and often as I like. My mind is still sharp. I am aware of everything around me. My body just moves slow and feels drained a lot."

BRIAN BOSWORTH

BRIAN BOSWORTH didn't like it when the Seattle Seahawks forced him to change his jersey number from his beloved 44 to 55, so he went to court. Bosworth's suit stated that there was an economic impact to the number change, as Bosworth had a corporation named 44-Boz Inc. And then there was the psychological factor. "The number thing might not mean a lot to others, but it does to me," Bosworth said. "I'm a very superstitious person. I thought it was discrimination against me."

It was a case of Brian Bosworth versus the Establishment. For a rookie linebacker in the National Football League, Bosworth had already put together an impressive streak of jousting with the Establishment windmill, and he had already been told by the Seahawks' coach, Chuck Knox, to keep his mouth shut.

Bosworth's legacy at the University of Oklahoma was nothing short of legendary. It began with his dual personality. Sometimes, he was Brian Bosworth, an above-average student with a steady girlfriend. At other times, he was "the Boz."

It was the Boz who—before the annual Oklahoma–Texas game—took on his home state of Texas, ripping apart its fans, its colors, and even its coach, Fred Akers. Then he came across with fourteen tackles as the Sooners romped.

There was the time the Boz admitted, while working at a job at the General Motors plant in Oklahoma City, that he had installed stray bolts in cars to rattle drivers.

And, of course, there was his suspension from the 1987 Cotton

Bowl, after he tested positive for use of steroids, which he said were prescribed by a doctor.

Did the Boz accept his punishment quietly? No way! Bosworth wore a T-shirt on which he came up with a new meaning for the NCAA (National Collegiate Athletic Association). He called it "National Communists Against Athletes" and added "Welcome to Russia." Despite the uproar that followed, Bosworth said he still wanted to play at Oklahoma. Although he had a year of college athletic eligibility left, he could have declared himself available to the NFL draft because he had completed his coursework. Barry Switzer debated openly whether he would accept Bosworth back. On one hand, he termed the 6-foot 2-inch, 240 pounder "beyond great." He added, "Comparisons are tough to make. But Dick Butkus ran a 5.0 forty [yard dash] and Boz runs a 4.6. He also bench presses 450 pounds. Believe me, that's a load of weight. And on the field, he dominates. He runs the show. He's been our leader since he was a freshman." On the other hand, the Boz seemed to him to be on the edge.

Bosworth also used his smarts to outmaneuver the Establishment in his move to the NFL. Instead of allowing himself to be chosen in the regular draft, and risk being assigned to a team for which he didn't want to play, he sat out the draft. He then called for a special supplemental draft and dictated the teams for which he would play. Seattle was not one of those teams, but after they dangled a ten-year, $11-million contract in front of him, Seattle became a mighty nice looking place to live.

For a while it appeared that the NFL version of Bosworth would be much tamer. After all, he admitted that the Boz was just a put-on that "got out of hand and took over Brian." He said, "So, I'm going to kill him and just be Brian, be me." But the vow didn't last long. Before the regular-season opener against the Denver Broncos, Bosworth threatened to go after Denver's star quarterback, John Elway, even if it meant risking a penalty. Seattle coach Chuch Knox quickly met with Bosworth and said, "Brian Bosworth was wrong. That's not Seahawk football. We're not out to inflict a career-ending injury on anybody." Bosworth then declined to be interviewed for several days.

The quiet didn't last long, for soon Bosworth's bout with the NFL over his jersey number occurred. The league said he had to wear a number in the 50s or 90s, as rules require of linebackers. But Bosworth, being Bosworth, was off and running at the mouth.

JOE NAMATH

IN ONE of the brashest statements ever made in the history of sports, Joe Namath not only predicted the New York Jets would beat the Baltimore Colts in Super Bowl III, he guaranteed it.

Years later the audacity and utter braggadocio of this statement might not be so apparent. But at the time they entered the game, the American Football League (from which the Jets emerged as champions) had lost the two previous Super Bowl meetings with the National Football League champions, the Green Bay Packers.

Although Namath was already proving himself in pro ball, the Colts had Earl Morrall, the NFL player of the year, at quarterback, with a backup none other than "The Master," Johnny Unitas. The Colts were expected to continue their NFL mastery easily and were installed as eighteen-point favorites. The final score was Jets 16, Colts 7.

Namath's predictions weren't the only outrageous statements he made before the big game. He provoked a response from Don Shula, then the Colts' coach, when he said that four AFL quarterbacks—including himself—were better than the Colts' Morrall. Shula responded, "He can say what the heck he wants, but I don't know how he can rap a guy like Earl. We're happy with Earl."

Namath's pregame talk also included a face-to-face meeting with the Colts' placekicker, Lou Michaels, in a Fort Lauderdale bar the Sunday before the Super Bowl. Rather than the near fight many newspapers reported, it was a sit-down affair. Michaels said later, "I thought from reading about Namath that he was a bum. But I found out he's a good kid. He told me that he was 'the greatest' and I told him he ought to learn one word—modesty. He said he was not interested in that word."

It seemed that Namath was interested in anything *but* modesty. He came out of the University of Alabama to sign the most expensive contract ever negotiated for a football player at that time (1965)—$400,000. He set himself up in an apartment in New York complete with llama rugs, circular bed, and mirrors on the ceiling, and invited the media in to view it all.

A magazine story written after the Super Bowl said Namath had spent the night before the AFL championship game in his apartment alternating between the white leather bar and a luscious young lady. The story went that the next morning Namath said goodbye to her with a pat on her rear, put on his mink coat, and went off to the game, in which he led the team past the Oakland Raiders and was named the most valuable player. Namath was asked about the article, and he said it was true except for two things: "The bar isn't white, and I wasn't wearing my mink."

The shining Namath star, however, seemed to be falling only months after his greatest moment. In June of 1969 a tearful Namath announced that he would retire from football rather than sell the New York bar, Bachelors III, in which he owned a share. Pete Rozelle, the NFL commissioner, said investigations had established that Bachelors III was frequented by disreputable persons, namely gamblers. The *New York Post* reported that a police official said, "The place was crawling with the worst sort of characters. We had men in there and there were all sorts of things going on. . . . It was a case of his [Namath's] not knowing what was going on. . . . But it was pretty bad." Six weeks later, Namath, whom the league had never accused of any wrongdoing, worked out a deal with Rozelle, sold the bar, and returned to pro football.

He was never able to get his team back into the Super Bowl. After several knee operations that drastically reduced his effectiveness, he spent his final season, in 1977, riding the bench with the Los Angeles Rams, before announcing his retirement.

Days before the announcement, the quarterback who had once shaved his Fu Manchu mustache for $10,000, waxed philosophical with reporters, including Skip Bayless of the *Los Angeles Times,* who wrote, "He came to Los Angeles the most famous football player of his time—No. 12, Broadway Joe, Super Bowl superstar, Joe Willie, White Shoes, Ol' Green Eyes, the World's Greatest

Lover, movie star, Johnny Walker Red, Fu Manchu, long hair, predicted victories, fast cars and women, fancy threads, Bachelor's III, pantyhose, Brut. "[He was] the man who helped free the thinking of close-minded conservative-thinking players and coaches everywhere. [He was] the quarterback some call the most talented ever to play."

When it was over, Namath even chuckled at the brash image he had left behind in 1969. "What was simple honesty most of the time or just refusing to accept somebody's bull, was misconstrued as rebelliousness," he said. But then he added, "Sometimes it may have been rebelliousness."

RIGGS VERSUS KING

WHAT WAS the biggest tennis match of all time? You could point to a McEnroe and Connors match, or perhaps one between Evert and Navratilova. But given the amount of time and money and attention it generated, you'd have to pick the match between Bobby Riggs and Billie Jean King.

When most tennis tournaments come to a finish, a live crowd of only a few thousand tennis fans is watching. But the eyes of the nation were on the Houston Astrodome on September 20, 1973. The match played to a crowd of 30,472—a Guinness record for one match—who paid from $10 to $100 for seats. There was a national television audience, for which ABC paid $750,000. And there was a purse of $100,000—winner-take-all.

The credit goes to the largest mouth in tennis, Bobby Riggs. Fifty-five at the time, Riggs had planted the seeds for his match with King by challenging and beating Margaret Court, another top woman player of the time. King, who had turned down earlier challenges, had had enough. "I can't just play for money," she said at a press conference to announce the match, billed the "Tennis Match of the Century." "I have to play for a cause, and I think the women were put down after Margaret played him."

Riggs used the two and a half months between the announcement and the match to keep up a steady barrage of verbal shots at King. His memorable statements included gems like:

"I'm glad to see her come out of the barn and play an old man";

"You've got the biggest mouth in women's tennis and I've got the biggest mouth in men's tennis";

"A woman's place is in the bedroom and in the kitchen, in that order"; and

"She expects to scrape me off the Astrodome floor. I will scrape her up. She is a woman and is subject to women's emotional frailties. She will crack up during the match."

The prematch excitement was overwhelming, breaking out of the sports pages of national newspapers. Bettors got into the act, too, and Riggs was installed as a 5–2 favorite.

The courtside crowd had banners proclaiming on one side, "Pigs for Riggs" and "I've Been Hustled by Bobby Riggs," and on the other, "BJ Is No. 1" and "Bobby Riggs—Bleagh!"

Once the ball began bouncing, King crushed Riggs, 6–4, 6–3, 6–4.

Rather than cry foul, Riggs said after the match: "I had to eat a lotta crow. I said a lotta things about Billie Jean before we played, and I have to take 'em all back now."

Weeks later, Riggs's mouth was back at it again. He even intimated that he had worked so hard promoting the match that he "just didn't have it" when it came to the competition.

He said, "Maybe as a fifty-five-year-old man, I may change the game. I could probably beat her in shooting free throws or in golf or in hitting softballs. Tennis is her own best chance to beat me, and she better stick to it."

Riggs never stopped looking for challenges. In 1984 he tried to challenge a list of top women golfers. Riggs said he would get to throw the ball once on each hole, rather than using a club. "I'm just a guy who likes to make a wager on almost anything," he said later. "It's been a way of life for me, and wherever I go, they practically line up around the block to play me at anything."

In 1985 Riggs, then sixty-seven years old, put together what he called his "last challenge." He and Vitas Gerulaitis, who had recently criticized the quality of women's tennis, played women stars Martina Navratilova and Pam Shriver. The match's purse: $300,000 to the winners, $200,000 to the losers. The women won, 6–2, 6–3, 6–4.

Riggs had lost again, but he wasn't crying—he was laughing all the way to the bank.

LARRY HOLMES

LARRY HOLMES will go down in the annals of boxing as one of the greatest heavyweight champions, whose career could have ended with a record-tying performance against Michael Spinks. Beating Spinks, in September of 1985 in Las Vegas, would have given Holmes a 49–0 record—tying the mark set by Rocky Marciano—and putting him in the same position as Marciano, who retired without a defeat.

But Spinks beat Holmes, in a close but unanimous decision, and rather than accepting defeat, Holmes lashed out against Marciano in the postfight minutes. "I'm thirty-five fighting young men, and he was twenty-five fighting old men—to be technical, Rocky Marciano couldn't carry my jockstrap," Holmes said. He also growled that the Marciano family was living off the memory of the late boxer. And he added that if he had hurt some of their feelings, that was too bad.

Instead of promoting sympathy, Holmes's remarks acted like a collective punch below the belt to all boxing fans. Dave Anderson, columnist for the *New York Times,* wrote, "The demon of his bitter ego has always been Larry Holmes's toughest opponent. . . . Now, sadly, Holmes will be remembered as much for his diatribe . . . against Marciano as he will for his seven-year reign. When he finally lost, he didn't know how to lose."

Holmes ended up apologizing for the remarks several days later; he called the Associated Press and said, "I want to offer my apologies to Rocky Marciano's family for remarks made at the press conference."

The damage to Holmes's reputation, however, had already been done.

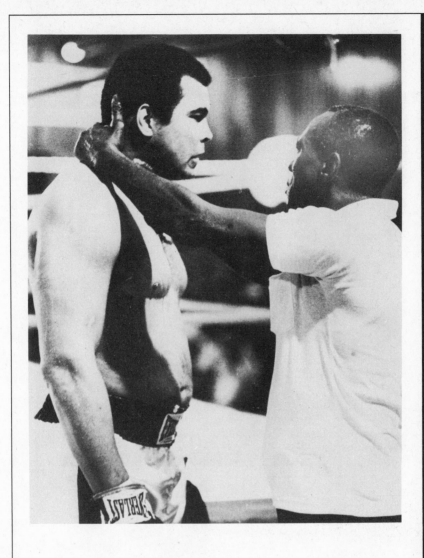

Muhammad Ali lets it all hang out during a training session for his 1976 match against Jean Pierre Coopman. (AP/Wide World Photos)

Oklahoma University linebacker Brian Bosworth announces his decision to go pro in May of 1987. (AP/Wide World Photos)

Joe Namath—no passing fancy

Bobby Riggs trains for his 1973 match with Billie Jean King. He says those 415 pills a day don't just give your strength, they sharpen your mind. (AP/Wide World Photos)

Billie Jean King displays her winning form during the famous match with Bobby Riggs. (AP/Wide World Photos)

Larry Holmes—his toughest opponent was his own ego. (AP/ Wide World Photos)

BRATS

MARY DECKER

JOHN McENROE

JIM McMAHON

SPORTS FIGURES I'D LOVE TO SLAP JUST ONCE...

Temper tantrums are to be expected in the high-pressure, high-visibility world of sports. But to be a brat, you have to cross that line and make a habit of complaining, bitching, and bawling.

MARY DECKER

MARY DECKER, lying on the side of the Los Angeles Coliseum track, grasping her side, her face a study in agony, is a picture etched in sports history. How did Decker end up being called the "unofficial crybaby" of the 1984 Summer Olympic Games? It had a lot to do with Decker's vindictive outburst toward Zola Budd, with whom she collided during the running of the 3,000-meter women's distance race.

There was a great deal of debate about who to blame for the collision. Decker, who holds most of America's women's distance records, didn't mince words. "I hold her responsible," she said in a postrace conference. "Zola tripped me. She cut in front of me and it was a matter of pushing her or me falling." By the next day, Decker still hadn't let up, and in a tearful interview on national television she continued to blame her opponent. As one writer put it: America's sweetheart had become America's sourpuss.

Who was responsible? A careful analysis of the video tape of the race provided no conclusive answers. The incident happened with slightly more than three laps (a little more than 1.25 kilometers) to go in the first 3,000-meter race ever held for women in the Olympics.

Decker and Budd, the eighteen-year-old South African turned Briton, were battling for the lead. Decker was on the inside and Budd was directly to her right. Coming down the straightaway, Decker appeared to give Budd a slight shove. Not long after, Budd extended her left leg to a point at about a forty-five-degree angle, and Decker tripped over it. Decker went sprawling and ended up being carried off the track. Budd went on to finish a disappointing seventh.

Afterward, Budd—who said she idolized Decker—denied she was at fault. Her attempts to apologize were waved off with a reported, "Don't bother" from Decker. Instead of sympathy, Decker's postrace performance drew barbs. One magazine, summing up the 1984 athletic year, wrote, "America's sorest loser—hands down."

In 1986 a much more composed Decker said that Budd had since accepted the blame for the trip. Looking forward to the 1988 Olympics, she was finally able to do a little gloating. "Now, all the people that put me down, who saw the great opportunity to rip me apart, they've got egg on their faces."

JOHN McENROE

THE TITLE of sports brat belongs to John McEnroe. In fact, "brat" isn't strong enough for some tennis observers; some people have called him a "superbrat." He's been called a "lout," "the pits," and a "moron," by the British press, an "embarrassment" by former tennis great Frankie Parker, and even a "jerk" by McEnroe himself.

It was after one of his celebrated on-court tantrums—this one with Vince Van Patten, who then accused McEnroe of trying to intimidate officials—that McEnroe said, "If I'm a jerk, I don't hide it, everyone knows about it. It is better than being a phony. I don't see what he has to complain about."

What *do* McEnroe's opponents complain about? Take July 4, 1980 for example, a semifinal match at the Wimbledon tennis tournament in England, where McEnroe has played some of his more memorable matches. A linesman yelled "out" on one of McEnroe's serves. McEnroe jumped two feet in the air and was livid. The umpire then reversed the call and called it a "let" with the point to be replayed. McEnroe stormed to the umpire's chair and began arguing that the ball was clearly in. The umpire refused to change the call, and McEnroe refused to play. When the play finally continued, McEnroe went on to win the set.

On the changeover of courts, McEnroe and Connors exchanged a few words. "My son is better behaved than you," Connors yelled. "I'll bring him to play you." Later in the match, when McEnroe again yelled at the officials, Connors barked across the net, "Shut up and play." The whole situation rang with irony. After all, here was a lesser McEnroe tantrum being met with admonishment from Connors, himself a former brat turned mellow middle-ager.

A year later at Wimbledon, an angry McEnroe hammered his racket on the turf after a call that went the opposite way. Further on in the match he hit the umpire's chair with his racket and called him an "incompetent fool."

He has broken rackets and lobbed balls into the stands. He has yelled, screamed, and pouted in major tournaments, and even in exhibition matches. Parker, a Wimbledon doubles champion with Pancho Gonzales in 1949, said of McEnroe's behavior, "They call the players ladies and gentlemen at Wimbledon, but he certainly hasn't been a gentleman. I think he does it for publicity, but he's a spoiled brat."

Why does McEnroe do it? He's been analyzed a million times by experts and critics, but even McEnroe himself admits he's not all that sure where it comes from. In a candid interview in 1985, he said he'd rather not be known as tennis's bad boy but conceded he had done little to change the label. "It's a frustrating thing," he said. "I feel my tennis outshines what I do otherwise. I don't go out to get people angry, but people love it when I get mad. It's just a spur-of-the-moment thing when I lose discipline. It's not really to get me going, it's just frustration that I show. Certainly some of it is my fault, but quite a bit of it is the press's fault. When we go into a place like Philadelphia, all you read all week in the papers is what spoiled, rotten people we are. They just dump all over us."

If he had to do it over again, McEnroe says he would do things differently. "It all started when I was eighteen at Wimbledon, and I was just a kid out of school then and didn't know anything. Now, it's hard to break what has already built up."

McEnroe did take six months off from tennis in 1986, and in the interim he and his wife, Tatum O'Neal, had a baby boy. And at a press conference called to mark his return to the game, he promised a new attitude.

The "new" McEnroe struggled to regain his form but ended up looking very familiar, particularly in a match in the 1987 U.S. Open, where an outburst cost him a fine and two-month suspension from the game.

He added at the time that he was upset, not just for himself, but because the incident disturbed his family and his wife, who was expecting their second child at the time.

JIM McMAHON

CHICAGO BEARS' football player Jim McMahon did not call the women of New Orleans "sluts" before Super Bowl XX, he does not wear sunglasses just to look cool, and he loves tacos.

Now that that's out of the way, let's get one sports columnist's honest appraisal of McMahon: at best he's obnoxious. Let's look at the famous "headband controversy" for the first bit of evidence. The headband he wore under his helmet clearly showed the word *Adidas* when he took his helmet off on the sidelines. Not coincidentally, that's one of McMahon's few sponsorship deals. The headband drew a wrist-slapping fine of $5,000 from Pete Rozelle, commissioner of the National Football League. Next came the Rozelle headband.

Don't forget the "acupuncture" headband he wore the days before Super Bowl XX, when he imported a specialist to help him relieve the pain he was suffering from a sore butt.

With his rear healed, he went on to give the New England Patriots a real pain in the game, hitting on twelve of twenty passes for 256 yards and running for another two touchdowns.

The victory propelled McMahon (who wears sunglasses because of a childhood eye problem) even further into the spotlight. The results were a Mad Mac poster, a bestselling book (replete with "outrageous" statements), and a series of commercials for Taco Bell.

Lest anyone think McMahon only became a pain when he became a pro, he was also called a "rebel" and a "one-man band in a quiet church" while at Brigham Young University.

The Irish Catholic kid born in New Jersey and raised in California found the Mormon lifestyle a bit stifling. At BYU, he said, "They make you feel like an alien—just because you're not one of them."

What does make McMahon tick? Mike Ditka, the Bears' coach, said succinctly, "He's different."

To some people his off-the-wall act is just that—an act, meant to capture the interest of the media. Steve Young, a teammate of McMahon's at BYU, said, "He might want to portray it that way, but he isn't that strange. No doubt about it, I think he enjoys the thought of somebody looking at him and saying, 'God, is that guy a little off, or what?' He's a father, a good husband, and a student of the game. He's not a flake or anything. I know better—he's not fooling me."

He has, however, fooled a lot of people. He managed to sling mud in all directions in his book. He ripped apart Michael McCaskey, the Bears' president, saying, "Michael McCaskey doesn't have any qualifications to run the Bears, except his name. . . . Most of us just laugh to keep from strangling him. . . . Michael McCaskey might think we won because of him; he'd be offended to learn that most of us felt we won in spite of him."

He slapped the rest of the NFL owners: "The owners, while they're testing for drugs, might want to test fellow owners. Not only for drugs, but for booze."

He wrote off teammate Willie Gault, stating, "Willie Gault is real pretty. . . . He's a former Olympic sprinter on his way to Hollywood, or so he hopes."

And he even badmouthed his parents, claiming, "I don't even feel comfortable around my own parents. . . . I suppose I'm the guilty one because I'm the only one of the children who didn't stay close to home."

McMahon, however, did not call the women of New Orleans "sluts." That remark was attributed to a New Orleans sportscaster who told television viewers the Wednesday before the Super Bowl that he had heard McMahon say, "All the women in New Orleans are sluts and all the men are stupid." The supposed McMahon comment set off a firestorm. McMahon's hotel room phone rang off the hook, the Bears' front office threatened a lawsuit, and the police rushed to the Bears' hotel to investigate a bomb threat. The sportscaster, Buddy Diliberto, later apologized, and his station management aired another apology, saying that they had no reason to believe the statements attributed to McMahon were ever made by him.

McMahon's next season was hardly tranquil. He came into training camp overweight and suffered a hip injury days into the camp. Then, in a September game against the Cleveland Browns, McMahon landed on his shoulder, signaling the beginning of a vexing problem to his throwing arm. That "problem" was pushed to the limit later in the season, in a game against the Green Bay Packers, when Packer defensive lineman Charles Martin slammed McMahon to the ground well after play had stopped.

McMahon suffered a slight tear in his rotator cuff, the group of tendons that hold the shoulder joint in place. Martin's hit, which cost the player a two-game suspension and $15,000, "made sure" that McMahon would need surgery, according to the quarterback.

McMahon was confident he would beat the one year timetable most doctors predict for rotator cuff comebacks, but he began the 1987 season on the injured-reserve list.

SPORTS FIGURES I'D LOVE TO SLAP JUST ONCE . . .

DANNY AINGE

JOAQUIN ANDUJAR

HOWARD COSELL

ILIE NASTASE

BILL LAIMBEER

THOMAS (HOLLYWOOD) HENDERSON

RICK BARRY

MARK GASTINEAU

DAVE KINGMAN

Mary Decker lies in agony on the track just moments after her collision with Zola Budd during the 1984 Olympics. (AP/ Wide World Photos)

John McEnroe

John McEnroe argues with an official at the 1984 Stella Artois tennis championship. (AP/Wide World Photos)

"What do you mean it's out?" McEnroe challenges a line judge at the 1983 Transamerica tennis tournament. (AP/Wide World Photos)

Jimmy Connors

Howard Cosell

Jim McMahon

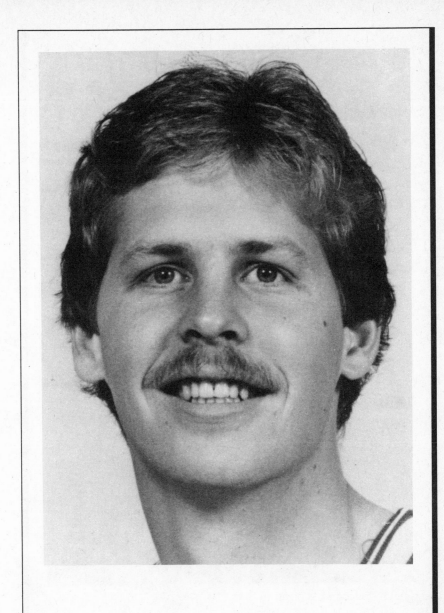

Danny Ainge

Dave Kingman

CATCHES

JOE NIEKRO

GAYLORD PERRY

ROSIE RUIZ

SMU

BLACK SOX

THE SOUTHWEST CONFERENCE

DARRYL ROGERS

A RACE TO COURT

BILLY HATCHER

In the sports world, the "win-at-all-cost" syndrome almost seems to say, "Go ahead, do anything you need to do to win. But don't get caught." It doesn't always work that way.

JOE NIEKRO

WHEN JOE NIEKRO was caught red-handed on the pitching mound in the middle of a game with an emery board, he took the classic defense: who, me cheat? Pitching for the Minnesota Twins against the California Angels on August 4, 1987, in Anaheim, Niekro was searched in the fourth inning of the game after the umpiring crew said it had noticed balls that had been scuffed in the same place. Scuffing a ball, or roughing the surface, is said to make the ball move more erratically as it heads toward the plate, making it harder to hit.

Niekro was ordered to empty his pockets on the mound. Surrounded by the umpiring crew, he flipped his back pockets inside-out, bringing his hands over his head in the process. But if this was supposed to be a magical disappearing act, it didn't work. The umpires saw an emery board lying on the grass, only a few feet from Niekro. Niekro was given the thumb and was eventually suspended for ten days.

The discovery hardly surprised the baseball world. California manager Gene Mauch said, "Nobody ever suspected Joe Niekro. Everybody always knew it. Those balls weren't roughed up. They were mutilated." Niekro, however, maintained his innocence, keeping a straight face in the process.

"I'll be honest with you, I always carry two things out there with me, an emery board and a small piece of sandpaper," said the forty-two-year-old pitcher after the game. "I've done that ever since I started throwing the knuckleball. Being a knuckleball pitcher, I sometimes have to file my nails between innings, so I carry an emery board with me to the mound."

Why the sandpaper? "Sometimes I sweat a lot and the emery board gets wet," he answered. "I used the other as a backup."

Niekro did not appeal his suspension. "If I've been illegal, I've been illegal for fifteen years," he said, several days after the incident. Umpire Dave Phillips, the crew chief, said the sandpaper taken from Niekro was "contoured to fit a finger. I'm sure he had it stuck to a finger in his glove hand. When we examined the sandpaper, there was a fingerprint on the back side."

Not everyone in baseball was so sure, though. Harry Dalton, general manager of the Milwaukee Brewers, said it would make perfect sense for a knuckleball pitcher to want to keep his fingernails groomed during a game. Others mentioned that if Niekro was scuffing a ball, he had to be doing it on the mound, and that no one saw anything suspicious.

At least one sports columnist noted that if Niekro was indeed scuffing the ball, he was doing a poor job of it. Entering the game, Niekro had a 6–8 record and a 4.38 ERA.

Niekro took the ten-day suspension in stride. He even made a guest appearance on "Late Night with David Letterman," ambling onstage with a carpenter's apron loaded with two bottles of Kiwi Scuff Magic, a tube of Vaseline, dozens of emery boards, sandpaper, tweezers, scissors, fingernail and toenail clippers, a nail file, and a clothes brush.

Baseball fans went along with the fun, too. At his first start after the suspension, in a game against the Tigers in Detroit, Niekro was taunted by fans holding emery boards, and several fans asked him to sign his autograph—on the back of their emery boards.

GAYLORD PERRY

DID HE or didn't he? No one in baseball seems to know for sure. It wasn't until August of 1982, with more than 300 victories and twenty years into his major-league career, that Gaylord Perry was ejected from a game for a violation of baseball rules 3.02 and 8.02. In other words, Perry was tossed for throwing a spitball.

It was the first time in the career of a player expected to be voted into the Hall of Fame that he was ejected for throwing a spitter—a pitch he admitted he once threw but said he no longer utilized.

The thumbing by umpire Dave Phillips left the forty-three-year-old Seattle Mariner furious. "No other umpire is as bad as Dave Phillips," Perry said. "He was heading for us. He was after the whole team. Phillips said it [the pitch] did something. It was a forkball."

Phillips said he had warned Perry about doctoring the ball in the fifth inning and ejected him two innings later—without looking at the ball. Phillips asked for the ball, but Seattle catcher Jim Essian threw it back. Phillips later added, "I'm not a chemist, but there was definitely a sticky substance on the ball. It came in like a fastball, and the bottom dropped out and it exploded. It was a classic illegal pitch."

After the incident, Perry was suspended for ten days. While several catchers who had been battery mates for Perry snickered that he had finally been caught, at least one former spitball pitcher—from the days when the pitch was legal—came to Perry's defense. Burleigh Grimes, baseball's last legal spitball pitcher, took the phone at eighty-nine years of age and boomed to a newspaper columnist, "It's absurd, absolutely absurd. How do they know? How do they prove it? They say the spitter is illegal because it's unsanitary. Tommyrot. What are they going to do—outlaw spitting? You might as well outlaw baseball."

Just what is a spitball and what does it do? Actually, a spitter can be doctored with much more than spit. A former catcher, Tom Haller, at the other end of Perry's pitches in the 1960s, said of the spitter, "It sinks. Most of the time you can see the difference because the ball drops sharply. It has a tendency to act like a sinker." Another former catcher said, "Usually the bottom drops out and then it breaks away from the hitter."

Another major league catcher during Perry's era, Rick Sweet, talked about what it takes to make a spitter. "You can use Vaseline, Firm Grip, which is a sticky substance, or just plain perspiration," Sweet said. "Even though I'm a catcher, I have experimented with throwing a spitter, and I've found that perspiration works the best. I've seen pitchers accidentally throw a spitter because they were sweating so much."

Sal Bando, another former major leaguer, said Perry has an advantage because he sweats a lot. "Gaylord has perfected the spitter to the point where he mixes it with Vaseline. I don't think it's fair for a pitcher to throw an illegal pitch. It's like a hitter putting cork in his bat. The spitter is dangerous."

Exactly what was Perry's technique? Gene Tenace, who caught Perry during a Cy Young Award–winning season with the San Diego Padres in 1978, said, "I can remember a couple of occasions when I couldn't throw the ball back to him because it was so greasy that it slipped out of my hands. I just walked out to the mound and flipped the ball back to him." Finally, Tenace said he asked Perry where he hid the substance he used to doctor the ball. "He told me to get away from him. He would never let me look at him."

ROSIE RUIZ

WHAT ARE the chances of a complete unknown winning the Boston Marathon? Sports reporters were trying to calculate the odds after an unfamiliar face crossed the finish line to win the women's division of the Boston Marathon in 1980. The woman was crowned with the traditional laurel wreath and champion's medal and led to the underground parking structure where the postrace press conference was held. Not one member of the press knew who she was, so one reporter cried out, "What's your name?" She answered, "Rosie Ruiz from New York."

She began to answer the questions put to her. Where did she work? Where did she live? Where did she train? How did she train? She answered them all but with none of the exhaustion the winner of a marathon usually shows. "I just wanted to finish," she said. "I didn't know I was the first woman until I crossed the line. To be sincere, this is a dream."

After the media session ended there were more questions than ever as another runner, Jacqueline Gareau of Canada, began questioning reporters about how Ruiz could have won. "I supposed I was first," she said in halting English. "The crowd kept yelling to me that I was first." Another runner, a male, said, "I heard the crowd cheering that Jackie was the first woman. I ran next to Jacqueline most of the way. And no woman passed me."

Reporters tried to find Ruiz, but she had gone, apparently as quickly as she came. Race officials quietly promised an investigation. Jock Semple, the crusty old fellow who had protected the male sanctity of the marathon in 1966 when he tried to push Kathy Switzer off the course, was less tactful. In his heavily accented voice, he swore at the absent Ruiz.

The story continued in the next weeks, and evidence piled up that Ruiz could not have run the race. A Florida author said that he had run with Ruiz the month before in Central Park in New York and struck up a conversation. Among the topics they discussed were how easy it would be to win the Boston Marathon without running it. The author told Ruiz that if she did it, she should give him a call and they could write a book about it. Two Harvard University students said that they saw a woman stumble out of the crowd and join the race a mile from the finish. When they saw the woman's picture in the paper the next day, she was called "the winner."

A year after she lost the title, Ruiz still insisted she had run the race. She said that she had had to avoid the press that year because of the "very difficult" time she was having. She also said that she changed jobs, apartments, received threatening phone calls, and had been sued for writing checks without sufficient funds.

Ruiz never ran again before big crowds, but she did continue to have her name in the news. In 1982 she was sentenced after a plea bargain to five-years probation on charges that she took $19,000 in checks and $5,100 in cash from an employer. And in 1983 she was arrested on charges of selling cocaine to undercover agents.

SMU

FOOTBALL HAD a proud tradition at Southern Methodist University. The school that produced Eric Dickerson, Don Meredith, Kyle Rote, and Heisman Trophy–winner Doak Walker lost a proud legacy in February of 1987. SMU—which had become the most penalized school in NCAA history—became the first institution to be hit by "the death penalty," a complete sports suspension.

The penalty was lowered on the school's football program by the NCAA for actions that occurred after the school was put on probation for three years in 1985. The violations the NCAA uncovered included a booster fund that paid thirteen players about $61,000, including eight players who received $14,000 after the 1985 penalty.

SMU's penalty sent shock waves beyond the Dallas institution, and a continuing furor over the violations and the penalties touched even the governor of Texas.

The penalty was SMU's fifth in twelve years. The NCAA's enforcement staff had recommended a lesser penalty, including the loss of nonconference games in the 1987 season. The NCAA infractions committee went much further and suspended the SMU football program in 1987, limited it to seven games, none at home, in 1988, and limited the number of scholarships in the 1988 season.

While the NCAA could have suspended the program for two years by its rules, observers felt the penalty would affect the program for a minimum of ten years.

"I think it effectively eliminates SMU from Division I-A football," said one commentator. "They may have to restart from scratch. And, with the highly competitive nature of Division I-A, that's pretty difficult."

Some people in the college football establishment reacted in horror to the penalty. "The decision is a disappointing one," said Frank Broyles, athletic director at Arkansas, who pointed to the school's work with the NCAA throughout the course of the investigation. "It seems the NCAA's sanctions against SMU are unduly harsh and signal to the rest of the NCAA's members that nothing can be gained by cooperation with the NCAA and it would be best for a member to stonewall any investigation."

The official SMU reaction was one of moderation: "We are disappointed at the outcome of the investigation and the judicial process with the NCAA." But at least one newspaper columnist openly criticized the NCAA for not going further. "Only in the cloud-cuckoo world of the National Collegiate Athletic Association could there exist a death penalty that lasts only one year," wrote Ron Rapoport of the *Chicago Sun-Times*. Rapoport continued, "Of all the violations of which SMU was found guilty, the one that follows is my favorite: After an NCAA infractions case had been settled in 1985, the athletic department continued to give illegal payments to the football players who hadn't been caught, while shutting out all newcomers without an under-the-table dime."

BLACK SOX

"SAY IT ain't so, Joe" is one of the most famous quotations in sports history. It was spoken at the conclusion of a trial following one of the most famous sports fixes of all time—the 1919 World Series.

The best-of-nine series was contested between the Cincinnati Reds and the Chicago White Sox—who, after the discovery that several members of the team were in on a fix, became known as the Black Sox.

Rumors of a fix began long before the final pitch was ever thrown in the series. Gamblers, it was later discovered, had paid off several members of the Sox, and the word spread quickly throughout the gambling underground, slowly surfacing to newspaper writers and even, some say, baseball officials, who did nothing to stop it.

In the first game, the money began to pay off, as Eddie Cicotte, the starting pitcher for the White Sox—and one of the players later identified as "bought"—allowed five runs in the fourth inning, as the Reds went on to win, 9–1. The Sox did win three games in the series, but Cincinnati took the eighth game, 10–5, to win the series, five games to three.

It wasn't until September of 1920, however, that an investigation began to uncover exactly what had happened. The subsequent trial was far from conclusive, as player confessions disappeared mysteriously before official proceedings began, and all players were acquitted. Baseball commissioner Kenesaw Mountain Landis, however, banned for life all the players supposedly involved in the fix.

The line attributed to a youngster waiting outside a grand jury chamber and uttered to Joe Jackson, one of the White Sox, was probably never spoken. It was a New York newspaper columnist, one of the most respected writers of the time, who wrote of Jackson's exit from the trial, saying, "He slunk along between his guardians, and the kids, with wide eyes and tightened throats, watched, and one, bolder than the others, pressed forward and said, 'It ain't so, Joe, is it?' Jackson gulped back a sob, the shame of utter shame flushed his brown face. He choked an instant, 'Yes, kid, I'm afraid it is. . . .' "

Jackson later said he had never talked to anyone except a deputy sheriff who bummed a ride from him after the trial. And Jackson's guilt itself is strongly doubted in the 1979 book, *Say It Ain't So, Joe* by Donald Gropman. Jackson himself was the inspiration for Bernard Malamud's *The Natural.*

Exactly who was in on the fix and who wasn't is open to debate. Jackson, it was pointed out, had twelve hits in thirty-two times at bat for an outstanding .375 percentage. And his versions of what happened differed greatly.

Still, a youngster's line and the tarnished Sox have made their mark on baseball history.

THE SOUTHWEST CONFERENCE

Fred Jacoby took over as commissioner of the powerful Southwest Conference in 1982.

Here's what his football-hungry kingdom looked like in mid-1987:

Southern Methodist—Hit with the "death penalty" for National Collegiate Athletic Association violations.

Houston—Under preliminary inquiry by the NCAA.

Texas—Slapped with a two-year probation without serious sanctions.

Texas A&M—Results of an internal investigation turned over to the NCAA.

Texas Christian—On a three-year probation through May, 1989.

Texas Tech—On a one-year probation through February, 1988.

DARRYL ROGERS

"They'll fire you for losing before they'll fire you for cheating."
—Darryl Rogers, Arizona State football coach

A RACE TO COURT

It took four years to decide who won the 1968 Kentucky Derby.

Dancer's Image, one of the prerace favorites, had finished a length and a half ahead of Forward Pass, another pick. But Dancer's Image was disqualified when traces of a drug were found in the horse's urine after the race. The drug was Butazolidin, described as an "aspirin" for horses, but also considered an illegal stimulant at that time in Kentucky races.

A four-year court battle ensued, in which both sides claimed victories on different levels. Eventually Forward Pass was installed as the winner, and the $122,600 purse, boosted by accumulated interest, was paid to the owners.

Peter Fuller, who owned Dancer's Image, ended up reportedly spending more than $250,000 in attempting to have his horse honored as the winner.

BILLY HATCHER

The winner of the "best excuses when caught cheating" contest is Billy Hatcher of the Houston Astros.

When Hatcher, an outfielder, cracked his bat during a game late in the 1987 season, it was found to have been drilled out and filled with cork. Ejected from the game, Hatcher said he would fight any suspension.

He claimed the bat belonged to one of his teammates, reliever Dave Smith. "I'm out of bats and grabbed one that was the same model," Hatcher said. "It was one the pitchers use during batting practice, and I had no idea it was corked."

Smith stated later that the bat was never meant to get into the bat rack for a game but was used as a joke in batting practice.

National League officials didn't laugh. They also didn't buy Hatcher's reasons, and he was suspended for ten days.

Joe Niekro

Joe Niekro asks, "Who me?" when he's accused of scuffing the ball during a 1987 game. (He was ejected when umpires found an emery board on the ground next to him.) (AP/Wide World Photos)

Gaylord Perry does his act. Did he doctor the ball during this 1982 game between the Seattle Mariners and the New York Yankees? (AP/Wide World Photos)

Rosie Ruiz, wearing the laurel wreath of the proclaimed winner of the women's division of the Boston Marathon (AP/Wide World Photos)

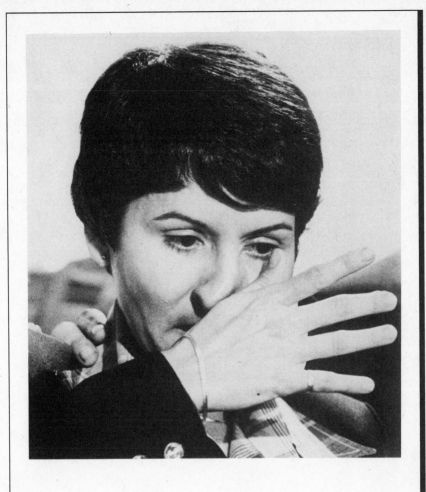

In a press conference held one week after the 1980 Boston Marathon, Rosie Ruiz still insists she won the race. (AP/Wide World Photos)

CRASHES

BILLY HAUGHTON

PELLE LINDBERGH

THURMAN MUNSON

STEVE PREFONTAINE

JOE THEISMANN

SHIRLEY MULDOWNEY

Success in sports can be deceiving. Top athletes often think they are impervious to injury. But life in the fast lane can also have its quick and inglorious endings.

BILLY HAUGHTON

He was called the Babe Ruth of harness racing drivers.

A thirty-five-year veteran of racing, with 4,896 victories and $39.5 million in purses going into 1986, Billy Haughton was, according to one driver, "the greatest in our business, an idol for everybody." Yet on Saturday evening, July 5, 1986, Haughton was killed during a race at Yonkers Raceway during an elimination heat. He was sixty-two years old.

According to wire-service reports, Haughton was behind Sonny Key, a two-year-old pacer, and moving at about thirty miles per hour when the horse collided with another in front of him. Haughton was catapulted from his sulky and landed on his seat; the momentum snapped his head back and off the ground. His head struck the ground so violently that his ineffective driving helmet split in half, and Haughton sustained a skull fracture that cost him his life.

Tragically, Haughton was only a week away from receiving a new, ultramodern helmet that was vastly superior to the model he was wearing the night of the accident. It was a helmet that some say might have prevented his death. The new helmet, like the old, was made of Fiberglas, but the newer model had a Styrofoam liner inside.

Ron Dancer, son of top trainer and driver Stanley Dancer, was head of the U.S. Trotting Association's helmet research committee for three years. He expressed frustration that the sport had not decided on a safer helmet earlier. "Of all professional sports, the only one that does not require helmets that meet a standard of safety is harness racing," Dancer said. "I don't know how many more tragedies there have to be before the USTA and the state racing commissions will take this issue seriously."

Days after the accident, Ron Dancer spoke of his father's friendship with Haughton, and he added that his father had shown Haughton a new helmet only days prior to the tragedy. "Just a week ago, I showed one to my father, who took it to the Meadowlands to show Billy," Ron Dancer said. "Billy really liked it and told my father to ask me to get him one. But the manufacturer told me the one I had was a prototype and that they were two weeks away from production."

Dancer said that after the accident he had had a talk with his father and asked him where the helmet was that he had shown Haughton. Stanley Dancer replied that it was in his locker at the Meadowlands. Ron Dancer then said, "I asked him, 'Will you wear it tonight?' One of the problems in this sport—in any sport— is that people get used to doing things a certain way. My dad's that way. Billy was that way. But he promised me he'd wear it. He'd better."

Another leading driver, Michel LaChance, who was driving a horse behind Haughton in the race, spoke about the danger of the sport. "Just talking about him makes my heart all funny," LaChance said. "People don't realize the dangers of this sport. We're moving at thirty miles an hour on these tiny, flimsy bikes. Imagine jumping out of a car at that speed. You also have 1,000-pound horses in front of you and behind you wearing steel shoes. If a punch can knock a man out, imagine what damage they can do."

PELLE LINDBERGH

ON NOVEMBER 14, 1985, ticket takers at the Philadelphia Spectrum took special care not to tear the tickets they were handling for the Flyers games against the Edmonton Oilers. On that night, as is the club's policy, the picture of a player appeared on the ticket, and by chance it was the turn of Pelle Lindbergh, the team's star goalie. The tragic irony, however, was that on this night fans at the Spectrum grieved at a fifteen-minute memorial service before the game for Lindbergh, who had been killed in a car crash earlier that week.

The crash occurred early in the morning, hours after the Flyers had beaten the Boston Bruins, a game in which Lindbergh, who had won the National Hockey League's Vezina Trophy as the top goalie the season before, had been rested and not played.

Lindbergh's bright red Porsche 930 Turbo, a prize possession whose speedometer went up to 190 mph, missed a turn on a winding road and smashed into a concrete wall in front of an elementary school. The native of Sweden, who fancied himself an exceptional driver and good enough to race professionally some day, was declared brain dead within hours, after having suffered extensive brain and spinal cord injuries. Two passengers in the car were injured but recovered. Apparently, none of the passengers was wearing a seat belt.

An autopsy performed later showed that Lindbergh had a blood alcohol count of between .17 and .24 percent. The legal limit for driving in New Jersey, where the accident occurred, was .10 percent.

Before his body was returned to Sweden, his family authorized several organ transplants, and his heart was given to a fifty-two-year-old father of three.

The Flyers' team physician said later that someone such as Lindbergh, who weighed 170 pounds, would have had to consume fifteen drinks within four hours to achieve a blood alcohol count of .24. "He had a fair amount to drink," said Edward Viner, the Flyers' team physician. "Pelle was not a drunk. He was a nice kid celebrating victory with a rare off day coming up."

Witnesses at the two bars where Lindbergh socialized before the accident denied he had had that much to drink, and a friend of Lindbergh's said that he had exchanged greetings with the goalie when he left the second bar, at about 5:20 A.M., and that he did not appear drunk.

Witnesses following Lindbergh's car out of the parking lot said that after starting off at about 30 mph, he "floored" the gas pedal and began speeding up, swerving at times into the opposite lane. After stopping at a red light, he pulled out fast again. Three-tenths of a mile after the stop light, Lindbergh encountered a treacherous turn near the Somerdale elementary school and the 3½-foot-high concrete wall next to the front steps.

Lindbergh didn't make it. Police reports said that he could have been traveling as fast as 80 mph and probably did not apply the brakes until he was within ten to twenty-five feet of the wall.

Bobby Clarke, the Flyers' general manager, said that Lindbergh was not a drinker and "hardly ever drank." Fighting back tears, he also described Lindbergh as a "bubbly little guy bouncing around the ice and fooling around in the locker room. Hopefully, something like this will change some of us." Clarke also acknowledged Lindbergh's driving habits. "He scares me. He's a fast driver. I don't think you buy a car like that to drive slow."

Lindbergh had posted a record of forty victories, seventeen defeats, and seven ties in the previous 1984–1985 season, and was named the Flyers' most valuable player and the NHL's top goalie.

In Sweden, where he was a national hero, one newspaper devoted thirteen pages to Lindbergh's crash and life. NHL fans didn't forget Lindbergh either, voting him to the position of starting goalie in the league's all-star game in 1986—the first dead man ever voted onto an NHL all-star team.

THURMAN MUNSON

THURMAN MUNSON was the grouch of the New York Yankees—
surly, cantankerous, and unapproachable. Yet when the plane
Munson was piloting crashed in August of 1979 and he was killed,
the whole baseball world mourned him.

The Catholic priest presiding at Munson's funeral in his home
town of Canton called Munson "a lovable grump who was something special." He continued, "Thurman was a very real person.
He knew what he wanted, and he worked hard to achieve it. He
was hard to get to know, but once you did, he was a great friend.
He died because he loved his family so much. Time was so
important to him. That's why he took up flying, so he could be
with his family as much as possible."

The list of funeral attendees read like a Who's Who of baseball
and included commissioner Bowie Kuhn and Yankees' manager
Billy Martin. Notes were read from Muhammad Ali and Reggie
Jackson, the same Reggie Jackson who, when traded to the Yankees
in 1977, said, "I am the straw that stirs the drink. Munson can't
do it." Jackson's remark, as one reporter put it, had left Munson
speechless, and forced him deeper into his shell.

Jackson attended Munson's funeral, however, and five years
later he wrote of the truce between them. "Our wars were behind
us by then [the time of the crash]. And if we weren't best friends,
I at least thought of us as battle-scarred comrades who finally
achieved a warm measure of respect and formed a basis of un-
derstanding."

Munson's death was a stunning blow to the Yankee organization, which had named him in 1976—the same year he was named the American League's MVP—its first captain since the legendary Lou Gehrig.

In 1976 Munson hit for a .302 average, and had 17 home runs and 105 RBIs as the Yankees advanced to the World Series (where they lost to the Cincinnati Reds).

The Yankees again won pennants in 1977 and 1978, beating the Dodgers in both World Series, but Munson was never completely happy and at one point asked to be traded to the Cleveland Indians to be closer to his Canton home, wife Diane, and three young children. The trade never materialized and Munson ended up purchasing a Cessna Citation, a million-dollar, twin-engine, eight-seat jet with the registration number 15NY. Munson wore the Yankees' No. 15.

It was on an off-day during the 1979 season that Munson, who had received his pilot's license only a short time before the crash, was practicing touch-and-go landings. According to reports, the plane crashed 1,000 feet short of the runway while trying to land at the Akron-Canton Airport. The plane lost its wings and burst into flames after the crash.

Munson, thirty-two at the time, was thrown forward upon impact. Because he was not wearing a shoulder harness, his head hit the instrument panel with enough force to dislocate his cervical vertebrae, leaving him paralyzed from the neck down. Unable to move, he could not help his two passengers when they attempted to remove him from the plane. Both passengers survived.

Munson died from asphyxiation due to the inhalation of superheated air and toxic substances, and acute swelling of the voice box.

Munson's widow later contended in a $42 million suit that Cessna had sold her husband a plane too complex for his training. In 1984 the suit was settled out of court for a reported $1.69 million.

An FAA field report, however, said the crash was caused by a startling number of mistakes by Munson. According to the report, Munson made a low approach and failed to correct for it; neglected to keep a close watch on the jet's air speed, letting it drop below a safe speed; forgot to lower the jet's landing gear, was reminded by a passenger to do so but then failed to compensate with enough power to overcome the added drag; and appeared to be unfamiliar with, or to have forgotten momentarily, the proper engine procedure for recovering from a low approach.

At his funeral, Munson's youngest son, four-year-old Michael, wore a replica of his father's uniform. It brought smiles through the tears. The real No. 15 was later retired by the Yankees, and Reggie Jackson wrote, "To this day, Thurman has never been replaced on the Yankees. Had he lived, I believe we would have won two more World Series in New York, both in 1980 and 1981."

STEVE PREFONTAINE

STEVE PREFONTAINE was called "the James Dean of the running set." He was, like Dean in life, a quick talker, gutsy, and aggressive. And Prefontaine was similar to Dean in death, too, a victim of an auto accident at the peak of his skills and with nothing but glory ahead.

On May 30, 1975, less than five hours after he had run the second fastest 5,000 meters in U.S. history in an NCAA meet, Prefontaine was killed.

Prefontaine, twenty-four, was alone in his sports convertible when it veered over the center line of a street in Eugene, Oregon, jumped a curb, smashed into a rock embankment, and flipped over, partially pinning him beneath the vehicle.

An autopsy showed Prefontaine had died from suffocation, because his chest was pinned under the weight of the car. "He couldn't have lived for more than a minute under the circumstances," said the medical examiner, "and he suffered no other injuries that would have caused his death themselves."

The autopsy also showed that Prefontaine was drunk at the time of the accident, with a blood alcohol level of .16 percent. Oregon law at the time said that over .10 percent was intoxicated, with a level of .15 percent or higher considered a criminal offense.

Prefontaine's death rocked the world of track, as friends and foes alike reacted to the news. Frank Shorter, who ran second to

Prefontaine in his final race, said, "I'm really upset. It's very hard to talk right now, it's very upsetting."

Others spoke about his style. Another runner and friend, Jon Anderson, said, "Nobody combined all the charisma, ability, and brashness. People were just drawn to him. There were probably twenty of us who gathered at Kenny Moore's house a couple of days after he died, and we decided nobody could call him a good or close friend. Pre lived his own style, and he was a tough guy to keep up with."

At 5 feet 9 inches and 145 pounds, he did not have the typical distance-runner build. When he once complained about having trouble with his weight, someone suggested he stop drinking beer. "I'd rather stop breathing," he retorted.

He was similarly outspoken about his goals—a gold medal in the Olympics and a World record—and why he ran. "To hell with love of country," he once said. "I compete for myself."

Prefontaine's brilliant career began at Marshfield High School in Coos Bay, Oregon, and he went on to win four consecutive NCAA titles. He qualified for the U.S. Olympic team in 1972 but finished fourth in the 5,000, vowing to return in 1976 to win a gold medal. Just before his death, he was named the most popular track athlete in the world by the respected *Track and Field News.*

His Olympic goal meant so much that he turned down a rich contract to join the professional track circuit to stay eligible, and his coach, Bill Dellinger, said, "There are a lot of very fine 5,000 meter runners in the world, and Pre definitely was one of them. This time, he would have been four years older. He would have four more years in strength and experience."

Three days after his death, a hearse wound around the track at Marshfield High before 2,500 silent people; it was Pre's final lap. More than a decade later, the track world still speaks of the legend of Steve Prefontaine.

JOE THEISMANN

FOR JOE THEISMANN, 1985 was the year of the crash.

First there was the end of his fifteen-year marriage to wife Shari, after Joe began spending more time with actress Cathy Lee Crosby. Then there was his career, which was sacked by New York Giants' linebacker Lawrence Taylor in November.

The crucial play occurred during the second quarter of the game. Theismann was caught behind the line of scrimmage by Taylor and another Giants' linebacker, Gary Reasons, who came over the top. Theismann's right ankle was twisted beneath him, and he suffered a compound fracture of the lower right leg. Taylor immediately jumped up and signaled for help, and Theismann was carried off the field on a stretcher.

At first, doctors were optimistic that the thirty-six-year-old Theismann would be able to resume his career after rehabilitation. But only days after the injury, Theismann needed further surgery, and doubts began surfacing about his ability to return. Sure enough, Theismann flunked his team physical the next season and was waived by the Redskins, after a pro career that began in 1971 in the Canadian Football League, and included two Super Bowl appearances with Washington.

But Theismann, never one to be shy with a microphone in his face, landed on his feet, signing on as a television broadcaster.

In 1987 he wrote his autobiography. His first wife—the two cut quite a social figure in their day—was never mentioned; Cathy Lee Crosby, whom he married after his divorce, got her own chapter, entitled "A Gift from Heaven."

110

SHIRLEY MULDOWNEY

- Broken pelvis
- Two compound fractures in her right leg
- Torn knee cartilage in her left leg
- Dislocated right ankle
- Severely sprained neck
- Every finger broken
- Thumb on right hand severed
- Left foot almost severed, found lying in her lap

These were the injuries suffered by former world champion Shirley (Cha Cha) Muldowney after the crash of her distinctive pink dragster during a qualifying run in an event on June 29, 1984, in Montreal.

An inner tube came out of her left front tire and locked the front wheel of her 3,000-horsepower dragster, sending her and her car off the drag strip and through a muddy marsh beside the track.

Only two years later, Muldowney was back racing.

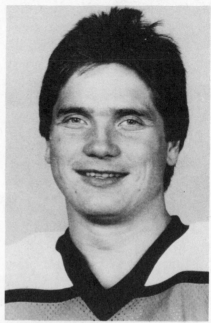

Pelle Lindbergh
(AP/Wide World Photos)

Pelle Lindbergh's car, shown after the crash that killed the star hockey goalie for the Philadelphia Flyers (AP/Wide World Photos)

Yankee catcher Thurman Munson's plane is examined after the fatal crash landing. (AP/Wide World Photos)

Thurman Munson

Distance runner Steve Prefontaine died when his sports car flipped over after he failed to negotiate a turn. (AP/Wide World Photos)

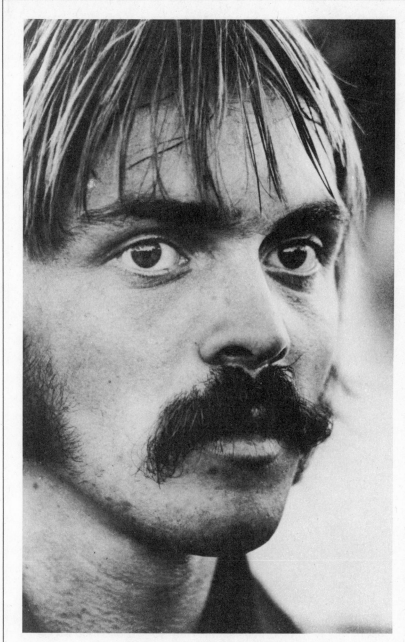

Steve Prefontaine (AP/Wide World Photos)

Washington Redskins' quarterback Joe Theismann is injured during a 1985 game against the New York Giants. (AP/Wide World Photos)

Lawrence Taylor

Shirley Muldowney

CRIMINALS

ORLANDO CEPEDA

BILLY CANNON AND JOHNNY RODGERS

DENNY McLAIN

MERCURY MORRIS

JOE PEPITONE

RACE CAR DRIVERS WHO TOOK THE LOW ROAD

QUOTES ON CRIME

Occasional mischief among athletes is usually met with a slap on the wrist. What school authority wants to bench the top quarterback, and what coach wants to hurt his team's chances to make the playoffs? But every once in a while an athlete will go too far and trade his uniform for a new outfit—prison garb.

ORLANDO CEPEDA

THE MOMENT Orlando Cepeda picked up two boxes at a Puerto Rican airport in 1975, he went from idol to outcast.

"People were afraid to talk to me," he was to say later. "They said I was Mafia and all that. They used to have pictures of me at the ball parks in Puerto Rico, but they took them away. The people say I'm a bad example to my boy and to their boys. Some day, people will know."

The two suitcases contained 165 pounds of marijuana—worth about $30,000—that Cepeda had helped smuggle into the country from Colombia. Cepeda said he did it for a friend. "No, it was not for money that I was about to lose my freedom, my honor, my good name," he wrote later. "I did it because my best friend asked me to, and I didn't have the strength to say no."

Cepeda did have a good name, a name that was rich with athletic tradition in Puerto Rico. His father Pedro was considered the greatest baseball player in Puerto Rico during his time, and was nicknamed "the Bull." His son Orlando was known as the "Baby Bull," even before he went on to make a name for himself in the American major leagues.

His major-league career started with a bang; he was named the National League rookie of the year in 1958 after hitting .312 with 25 homers and 96 runs batted in. Shifted from first base to the outfield, he played nine seasons with the San Francisco Giants before he was traded to the St. Louis Cardinals in 1966. The next season he was the National League's MVP, hitting .325, with 25 homers and 111 RBIs, and helped the Cardinals to the World Series.

A deformed leg finally hastened the end of his career. He was shipped to the Atlanta Braves, Oakland As, and Boston Red Sox before ending his career with the Kansas City Royals at the age of thirty-seven in 1974.

He returned to his homeland a hero, with plenty of money and plans to open his own business. But he found out after his sentencing for possession of marijuana and illegal transportation of drugs that the bigger they are, the harder they fall, and, while in prison, he accused the Puerto Rican criminal justice system of making an example out of him. Sentenced to two years in prison, he served only ten months, but the damage to his reputation seemed irreparable.

In 1980 he surfaced in Chicago as a batting coach for the White Sox. There he said, "I never thought I'd be back in baseball. When I retired I wanted to set up a health spa in Puerto Rico. But all my plans went down the drain. I don't dislike anyone for what happened to me. It was part of life, and I'm just going to go on and try to be happy."

After an unpleasant season with the team, he again returned to Puerto Rico and opened a baseball school for youths. He said he volunteered several times, to no avail, to help the major leagues warn young ball players about the dangers of drugs.

BILLY CANNON AND JOHNNY RODGERS

IN 1983 Billy Cannon discovered that the Heisman Trophy may be the most prestigious individual award in all of sports, but it isn't big enough to hide behind in a courtroom. Johnny Rodgers was reminded of this in 1987, when the Heisman Trophy was sitting in front of him on the defense table. San Diego Judge Jack Levitt said, "Mr. Rodgers is not a very stable individual. He's not a truthful individual. I don't think he should have gained any credit for winning the Heisman Trophy, nor should he have gained any detriment by it. I think he's ridden that horse way too long." With that, Levitt packed Rodgers' saddlebags for a six-month stay in jail after he was convicted of assaulting a cable television technician with a pistol.

Cannon's downfall was more spectacular. In 1983 the former LSU superstar was charged with masterminding a scheme in which $1 million in one-dollar bills was counterfeited. A prosecuting official called the case one of the largest of its kind in the country.

Years earlier there had been other, more flattering, superlatives for Cannon, particularly after a game against Ole Miss in 1959. Then a senior, Cannon took a punt and ran it back eighty-nine yards for a touchdown to give his team a 7–3 lead in the final quarter. The play, according to one newspaper, was "one of the great runs in all the annals of sport." It elevated Cannon from the level of an outstanding player to a "legend."

At season's end, Cannon easily won the Heisman balloting with 1,929 points. Richie Lucas of Penn State came in second at 613, and third was "Dandy" Don Meredith of SMU at 286. And who should end up handing Cannon his trophy but then Vice-President Richard M. Nixon, who said the running back was "not an ordinary cannon, but an atomic cannon."

So valuable were his services thought to be that the AFL and NFL each said they had him signed to valid contracts. A judge ruled in favor of the Houston Oilers of the AFL, and Cannon—pro football's first $100,000 player—went on to an eleven-year career in the league. After his retirement, he became a successful orthodontist in Baton Rouge, Louisiana.

His exploits were not forgotten. In 1982 he was named to the college football Hall of Fame, but before he could be inducted, he was indicted, when a cache of counterfeit bills was found buried on his property.

Records showed Cannon had lost a $122,000 condo because he couldn't keep up payments, and that he was under a court order to pay $246,000 on a promissory note when he was arrested.

Cannon pleaded guilty and ended up serving three years of his five-year sentence before being released in 1986.

He was never inducted into the Hall of Fame; the hall's executive board turned down his nomination after his arrest.

Rodgers' demise, while less spectacular, was more predictable. His brilliant career at Nebraska was punctuated by game-time heroics and off-the-field capers, including a gas station robbery his freshman year—he called it a prank—which netted him two-years probation.

Observers, however, still liked what they saw. Dan Jenkins wrote in *Sports Illustrated,* "In terms of size, Johnny Rodgers has to be the most devastating player who ever suited up at no more than 5-foot-9 and 173."

As his field prowess grew, his problems did not let up. There was an arrest for possession of marijuana. There were numerous police visits to his apartment—harassment, he called it.

When Rodgers won the Heisman his senior year, it was enough to prompt Jim Murray, the *Los Angeles Times* columnist, to write, "Somewhere along the line, I had gotten the idea the Heisman Trophy was for more than athletic excellence . . . the idea he had to have a little Frank Merriwell in him. . . . I don't mind that this year's winner has knocked over a gas station. Anybody can do that. It's his public utterances that stop me, not what he does in private."

Rodgers went on to play four years in the Canadian Football League, before spending three seasons with the San Diego Chargers, where his career ended in 1979.

He was arrested in October, 1985, after an incident in his San Diego home where he pointed a pistol at a cable television technician who had arrived to disconnect service for nonpayment. The charges were assault with a deadly weapon and being an ex-felon in possession of a firearm.

During the trial Rodgers acted as his own attorney after claiming he was unhappy with the work done by his previous five lawyers. Judge Levitt found Rodgers in contempt twice for statements he made about the Heisman Trophy and about being pardoned for the 1970 robbery conviction.

With the fifty-five-pound Heisman on the defense table to "watch" the whole proceeding, he was sentenced to spend six months in jail. The judge said that he opposed probation because he saw no remorse, and he believed that Rodgers misrepresented facts while acting as his own attorney.

DENNY McLAIN

AFTER A twelve-year absence from the pitching mound, Denny McLain took the hill again in the summer of 1985.

This time his audience was armed guards, who were there to make sure that only baseballs—not people—went over the walls. McLain's new bullpen was in a federal penitentiary in Atlanta. A former winner of the Cy Young Award, McLain was wearing prison blues instead of pinstripes as part of a twenty-three-year sentence for gambling and drug charges.

After two splendid seasons McLain's career had plunged. In 1968 he led the Tigers to the AL pennant, posting a 31–6 record and winning the AL's MVP and Cy Young awards, and in 1969 he had a 24–9 record and shared the Cy Young Award with Mike Cuellar. But in 1970 McLain was suspended for alleged involvement in bookmaking three years earlier. Reinstated later in the season, he was traded to the Washington Senators, then dealt to the Oakland As in 1971, before ending his career with the Atlanta Braves in 1972.

McLain was also suspended at other times during his career, once for carrying a gun, and again for throwing a bucket of water on two sports writers.

McLain spent the time after his retirement heading a musical combo, acting as general manager of a minor league team, and running a mortgage company, before going into the medical clinic business. He remained a fan favorite and was invited back to Tiger Stadium in 1982 to receive replicas of his MVP and Cy

Young awards (the originals had been destroyed in a fire several years earlier). At that time McLain said, "The only thing I wanted to salvage from the fire were those awards. Those three awards had a lot of meaning to me personally."

During his trial, puffy-faced and grossly overweight, McLain testified to a gambling habit; he would sometimes spend $5,000 a night betting. He admitted getting involved with bookmaking but denied the other charges.

The government accused McLain of being part of a loan-sharking operation that charged interest rates of 130 percent, used threats to collect, and booked high-stake bets on professional and college football and basketball games.

McLain was also accused of possessing 13 kilos of cocaine and planning to smuggle 400 kilos of cocaine from Colombia.

McLain's courtroom pitch was less effective than his fastball. He was found guilty on racketeering, extortion, and cocaine possession charges and was sentenced to twenty-three years in prison.

In 1986 McLain's name surfaced again. Sources said that McLain was thrown in the hole (a solitary confinement unit) for telling lawyers that the prison had used library money to buy books such as *Erotic Aerobics* and videotapes such as *Little Miss Innocence.*

McLain was later transferred from Atlanta to a prison in Terre Haute—closer than ever to Detroit, his place of glory.

In 1987, McLain's conviction was overturned by a federal court of appeals. But he said it was unlikely he'd be back in baseball soon. "I'm not sure baseball is ready for Dennis McLain yet."

MERCURY MORRIS

His NICKNAME was Mercury, and he was indeed swift of foot.

But on August 16, 1982, Eugene Edgar Morris, whom National Football League fans knew as Mercury, wasn't fast enough to evade law enforcement agents in Miami. Morris, who later admitted to being a cocaine addict, was arrested and charged with trafficking in drugs, as he played the part of a middleman in the sale of 456 grams of cocaine to an undercover agent.

The Mercury Morris who made the sale was far from the same man who had played and earned three Super Bowl rings for the Miami Dolphins and set numerous Dolphin club records. Broke and desperate to "put food on the table" for his family, including a wife, daughter, and two sons, and admittedly needing to continue his cocaine habit, Morris agreed to act as the middleman in a sale arranged through the help of his former gardener. The gardener turned police informer, claiming Morris owed him money.

Morris, who ended his NFL career in 1977, had exhausted his life savings. A $55,000 speed boat and $250,000 in the bank were gone. His Super Bowl rings had disappeared, and he cannot remember if they were lost, stolen, or traded for cocaine. Foreclosure proceedings had begun on his home.

Law-enforcement agents had bugged the cocaine buyer going to Morris's home and tapped his phone. When the agent identified himself, Morris took the bag of cocaine and tried to throw it into the canal behind his home. The bag hit the fence; he grabbed it and threw it again. This time it went over, but it did not sink and was soon recovered.

Police also confiscated several weapons and $124,000 in cash along with the drugs. Morris's profit on the deal would only have come to $1,000. While admitting to his part in the deal, Morris blamed the government for turning him into a trafficker. What turned him into an addict?

Morris pointed to an injury suffered during a Monday-night football game with the Pittsburgh Steelers in 1973, when he came out of the backfield, took a short pass, and was immediately tackled by Steeler cornerback Mel Blount. Morris said that as he hit the ground, he felt the worst pain in his life. Weeks later it was discovered that two vertebrae were broken in his neck. An operation was performed, but two years later, he said that he had reinjured his neck in a car accident and begun having "horrible headaches." He thought of suicide, but instead turned to cocaine and began freebasing the drug.

Only weeks before his arrest he had begun counseling to turn around his life.

Morris refused to plea bargain, and after the trial he was sentenced to twenty years in prison.

The prosecutor, George Yoss, said, "I rooted for Mercury Morris in 1972 and 1973, but now he has to pay the price. I understand what he's gone through. But none of that takes away the fact that he was trying to earn money selling cocaine on the streets of Dade County."

Morris began serving time in prison, but after three years the Florida Supreme Court ordered a new trial on the grounds that Morris's lawyers were not allowed to show evidence of entrapment. While awaiting the new trial, he entered a no-contest plea of one count of conspiracy to traffic drugs, and as part of the plea bargain, prosecutors dropped three other charges. He was then sentenced to four and a half years in prison and was credited with having served three and a half with one more year credited to him for good behavior.

The same judge who had sentenced him to twenty years in jail, congratulated him on his work to combat the drug problems in Florida, which he began while in prison. In the months after his release, Morris began lecturing on the evils of drugs.

JOE PEPITONE

"I FIND it particularly sad when someone who graced New York in Yankee pinstripes will now have to serve his time with the New York Department of Correction in prison stripes." After these ironic words, a New York judge sentenced Joe Pepitone to six months in jail on two misdemeanor drug convictions in 1986.

Yet it could have been worse. Pepitone and two other men were arrested in March of 1985 after their car was stopped by police in Brooklyn. The list of items taken from the car included the following: more than a kilo of cocaine, Quaaludes, drug paraphernalia, glassine envelopes, records of drug transactions, and a loaded handgun.

Pepitone was acquitted of the more serious charges, and that was typical Pepitone—never quite living up to expectations. Indeed, the title of Joe's autobiography was *Joe, You Could Have Made Us Proud.* As a youngster he was touted as the next "hope" of the Yankees. He ended up being one of the team's biggest disappointments.

After signing for a huge $25,000 bonus in 1962, Pepitone, a first baseman and outfielder, played with the Yankees for eight seasons. His batting average, however, never reached .275, and he was known more for his hairstyle and off-the-field swinging than his playing.

His departure from the Yankees brought a chorus of philosophers. Joe Garagiola, player-turned-broadcaster, said, "He's the kind of player who, if he breaks his comb between games of a

132

doubleheader, can't play the second game." Columnist Joe Durso called him "the last and most controversial of the old imperial New York Yankees." And Lee MacPhail, then the team's general manager, said, ". . . it'll be hard to imagine the Yankee club without him. He's been a real good player, but not as good as everyone hoped he'd be. He was colorful and he had the spirit of youth, and some of the problems that go with it."

Pepitone himself put it a bit less diplomatically, saying, "I wanted a different girl every night, one after another, after another, after another. And every conceivable type: blacks, whites, Puerto Ricans, Chinese, Indians, Serbo-Croatians . . . you name it, I'd surely love to try it."

After the Yankees traded Pepitone, his career continued with three different teams and four sporadic seasons.

He retired after seventy-five games with the Astros and then was "rescued" by Chicago Cubs' manager Leo Durocher, hitting a career high of .307 in 1971. In 1972 he retired again, only to return a few months later. He was traded to the Atlanta Braves during the 1973 season, but after a matter of days, he quit and signed on with a Japanese team and ended his playing days overseas.

In the late 1970s, Pepitone played in and managed a pro softball league. He told a reporter who caught him at home late one night, "I'm sitting at home, in front of the fireplace. It's a little chilly here and my son and I were watching the Yankee game. I'm thirty-eight years old now, babe. I've straightened out most of my problems. I'm married, I stay home, I don't fool around anymore."

Pepitone returned to the Yankees briefly as a batting coach but did not make headlines in New York again until his arrest in 1985.

At his sentencing the forty-six-year-old Pepitone heard the judge say, "At one time Mr. Pepitone was a star first baseman with the New York Yankees. Once a first-rate baseball player, he now stands before the court a second-rate drug operator."

RACE CAR DRIVERS
WHO TOOK THE LOW ROAD

John Paul Sr. was already serving twenty years for hiring a hit man to murder a federal witness and still faced numerous other charges when he added to his stay in a Florida prison in March of 1987 by taking part in an escape attempt. Paul and a fellow inmate walked up to a guard and squirted a mixture of hot sauce and disinfectant in his face. The guard was wearing glasses, however, and before the two men could get to the top of the fence and over to a waiting pickup truck, he recovered and fired a warning shot. The two climbed down and were sent to solitary confinement.

Paul and his son, John Paul Jr., were accused of bringing 200,000 pounds of marijuana into the United States between 1975 and 1983.

Before their downfall, Paul Sr. and his son had won five straight Camel GT titles in 1981 and 1982, and Paul Sr. had twice won the World Endurance Drivers Championship.

He was arrested in Switzerland in 1985 after fleeing the country and forfeiting $500,000 in bail, and he was convicted of hiring a hit man to kill a federal witness prepared to testify against him. In 1986 John Paul Jr., the winner of the 1983 Michigan 500 race, was sentenced at the age of twenty-seven to a minimum of five years in prison after plea bargaining on a racketeering charge.

Randy Lanier was the rookie of the year in the 1986 Indianapolis 500. Later that year he was indicted for drug trafficking and fled the country. Lanier, who finished thirteenth in the Miami Grand Prix in 1986, was said to be either in South America, or dead.

Bill and Don Whittington were a brother act. Bill was sentenced to fifteen years in prison in 1986 after pleading guilty to laundering money from a Colombia-to-Florida marijuana smuggling operation during 1977 to 1981. A five-time Indy 500 entrant, he won the 24 Hour of Le Mans race with his brother Don in 1979. Don Whittington only received an eighteen-month term after pleading guilty to filing a false income tax return and attempting to defraud the IRS.

Salt Walther, the veteran Indy car driver, in 1987 faced charges in Indiana for drugs, and in Ohio for writing worthless checks.

QUOTES ON CRIME

"If it is a cliché to say athletics build character as well as muscle, then I subscribe to the cliché."
—Former President Gerald R. Ford

"Make no mistake. Professional football frequently shines brightly as the great American sport. But at other times, it just out-and-out stinks. And there is merit, I believe, in showing it in both aspects."
—Former pro football player Johnny Sample

"Baseball tries to keep its straight image; that's a lot of bullshit."
—Former baseball star Orlando Cepeda

"I can't believe I'm here. The Cuban Cowboy in a place like this. Shit. Not being free, that's the worst. I see men crying in here, I see so many men desperate. I'm so lonely, too. Maybe I'll contact some big-league clubs when I get out. But in the meantime, it's so bad here. Most nights, I'm also crying myself to sleep."
—Former New York Yankee Pedro Ramos (from a cell in a Florida prison where he was doing time for possession of drugs and a weapon)

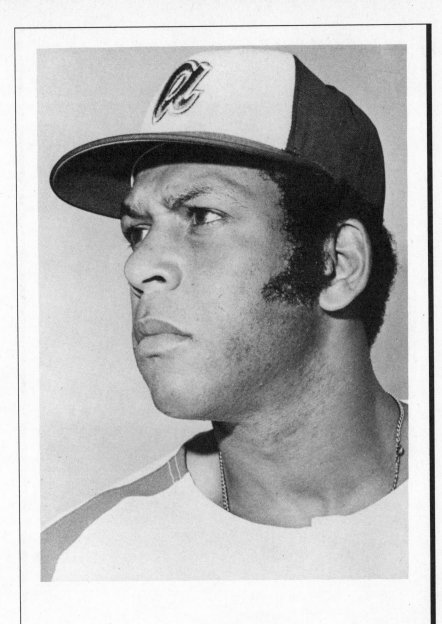

Orlando Cepeda

Billy Cannon after sentencing (AP/Wide World Photos)

Johnny Rodgers shows off his 1972 Heisman Trophy. (AP/Wide World Photos)

Johnny Rodgers after he was sentenced for assault (AP/Wide World Photos)

Denny McLain's special license plates refer to his 31–6 record in 1968. (AP/Wide World Photos)

Denny McLain is led from the Tampa courthouse in handcuffs.
(AP/Wide World Photos)

Mercury Morris

Joe Pepitone is booked at a Brooklyn police station after his arrest on drug and weapon charges. (AP/Wide World Photos)

John Paul Jr.

Randy Lanier

Don Whittington

Bill Whittington

FIGHTS

TEDDY GREEN VERSUS WAYNE MAKI
BILLY MARTIN
RUDY TOMJANOVICH
JOHN MATUSZAK
KEN PATERA
WOODY HAYES
FIGHTING WORDS
SOCCER RIOTS TO REMEMBER

"Boys will be boys," as the saying goes. While brawls on the playing field are not treated the same way as brawls in the barroom, the results can sometimes be as tragic.

TEDDY GREEN VERSUS WAYNE MAKI

TRYING TO pick out the worst hockey fight of all time is like trying to decide on the worst car crash of the last twenty years. Where do you begin?

Here's one vote for a fight that ended not in the penalty box but in a courtroom, with one player thankful he even lived to stand charges.

It was September 21, 1969, in Ottawa, Canada, and the NHL exhibition game featured the Boston Bruins and St. Louis Blues, with Teddy Green, the rugged Bruin defenseman, squaring off against St. Louis's Wayne Maki.

Green had previously earned the nickname "Terrible Teddy" on a club nicknamed "The Animals." He was quick to use his fists and not averse to using his wooden stick for combat.

Descriptions of the fight were somewhat sketchy, but Green and Maki had apparently wiggled their sticks at each other. Maki rapped Green, Green rapped Maki, and after Green turned away to break off from the incident, Maki got up from the ice, lifted his stick over his head, and smashed it down on Green's unprotected skull.

Green went down, bloody and suffering from a fractured skull, and was immediately hospitalized. His injury required the insertion of a metal plate in his skull and two operations, and he suffered some temporary paralysis on his left side.

During his hospital stay, Green sent word to the NHL hierarchy that he would like to see stick swinging come to an end. Milt Schmidt, the team's general manager, said, "In Teddy's own words, 'After being through this thing myself, I never want to see something like this happen to anyone else.'"

The NHL did indeed send out an order to referees to crack down on ice violence. Scotty Morrison, the league's referee-in-chief, said that refs were to be instructed to "rule with an iron hand." And he said that if any player swings at another's head, it would cost the player a match penalty, even if the players were ten feet apart.

At about the same time as his hospital proclamation, Green received a bedside greeting from the NHL: he was suspended for thirty days and fined $300, with the suspension to be deferred until he was well enough to play. Maki received the same fine.

The two shared in another similar message when criminal charges were filed in Ottawa by the district attorney—the first time in NHL history that players were brought up on criminal charges. Both men were charged with assault and committing bodily harm. Convictions on the charges carried a maximum of two years in prison. The cases actually went to court, but both players were eventually acquitted.

Green recovered from his injury and was judged fit to return to play. Maki retired from hockey during the 1972–1973 season because of a brain tumor. He died in 1974 at the age of twenty-nine, leaving a wife and two children.

In 1987 the NHL was still attempting to crack down on violence with a new set of "get-tough" rules.

BILLY MARTIN

BILLY MARTIN'S record as a battler on the field is eclipsed by only one other aspect of his fiery life—his list of off-the-field fights. In fact, Martin might be the all-time sports brawler. You'd need both hands and feet to count the number of fights where Martin has received publicity, from his first brawl as a player in 1952, to his recent but short two-rounder with player Ed Whitson, who ended up breaking Martin's arm.

Martin's first fight was with Jimmy Piersall, then a member of the Boston Red Sox, on a ramp under Fenway Park in 1952. Piersall ended up with a bloody nose. He was shipped to the minors two days later and two months later was hospitalized with severe mental depression. Martin later apologized, saying, "I didn't know he was sick, otherwise I never would have gone after him."

Martin's other victims included Clint Courtney, a player with the St. Louis Browns, in 1952 and again in 1953; Tommy Lasorda in 1956; Jim Brewer in 1960; and marshmallow salesman Joseph N. Cooper in 1979.

No fight Martin was ever involved in had as much significance for his career as one in which Billy claimed he never threw a single punch—the fight known as the "Copacabana Incident."

It was the 1957 season, a season in which Martin had started off with a warning from Yankees' official George Weiss, "Keep it clean or you are gone." Martin's luck, however, and his career with his beloved Yankees, lasted only until mid-May that season. It was May 15, an off-day for the Yankees, when Martin promoted a birthday celebration for teammate Yogi Berra, whose birthday had been the 12th. (Martin's birthday was the 16th.)

Martin went alone and was joined by Berra, Mickey Mantle, Whitey Ford, Hank Bauer, Johnny Kucks, and their wives. Dinner was held in the quiet atmosphere of Danny's. Then the group moved on to the Waldorf, where they heard Lena Horne perform. When the wives decided they would like to end the evening by hearing Sammy Davis Jr. at the Copa, Martin obliged and reserved a table for the group for the 2 A.M. show.

Seated next to the players' table was a large group full of league bowlers who were celebrating another championship. The bowlers, who had been drinking heavily, began harassing Davis during his show. The harassment continued, and the bowlers tried to engage the players in a conversation. Finally, Davis stopped his musical accompaniment and walked over to the bowlers, telling them either to keep quiet or leave.

One bowler said, "Goddamn nigger trying to tell me what to do." Bauer again told the group to keep quiet or leave. The man, later identified by police as Edwin Jones, a deli owner from Manhattan, allegedly said to Bauer, "Why don't you make me?"

Bauer, quickly aroused to anger, got up from his seat and began following Jones into a small alcove area. Martin, too, got up, and got into a verbal battle with Jones's brother, Leonard.

By the time the two looked around, Edwin Jones was already lying on the floor, the victim of a concussion, a possible fractured jaw, and skull injuries. Bauer later said, "I didn't hit anybody. If anybody was hit, it had to be the bouncers who did it." Mantle wrote in his book, *The Mick,* "I know this. Bauer never laid a hand on anybody. Neither did Billy."

Gossip columnist Leonard Lyons of the *New York Post* happened to be across the street and rushed to get the story. The headline in one of the next day's papers said, "Yankees Brawl in Copa." A grand jury was convened, at which Berra was quoted as saying, "Nobody did nothin' to nobody."

No one was charged, but Weiss was furious at Martin for having led the rest of the team astray. And on June 15, the day of the trade deadline, Martin was shipped to the Kansas City Athletics in a seven-player deal that brought pitcher Ryne Duren and outfielder Harry "Suitcase" Simpson to the Yankees.

It was the beginning of what was to be a long odyssey for

Martin. A twenty-nine-year-old infielder in decline, Martin ended up with five more teams in the four seasons he had left in his career. His playing days ended with another famous fight, this time with Jim Brewer, who was then a rookie pitcher with the Chicago Cubs.

Brewer threw a tight pitch that sent Martin sprawling to the ground. The next pitch was wide, but Martin swung anyway and ended up sailing his bat toward the mound. Martin, a smile on his face, slowly went after his bat, and Brewer deliberately walked off the mound. "I saw his fist cocked and I punched him," Martin said.

A brawl ensued, emptying both benches. Brewer ended up with bruised ribs and a broken bone under one eye, an injury that could have cost him his sight. Martin claims he never hit Brewer; witnesses swear that Cal McLish, Martin's teammate, seemed to be the player who landed the most punches on Brewer's face. But it was Martin who was fined $500 and suspended five days without pay, and who was later sued for $2 million by Brewer and the Cubs. Martin replied, "Ask Mr. Wrigley how he'd like it, cash or check."

Martin later ended up paying Brewer $10,000, but he never stopped fighting.

RUDY TOMJANOVICH

WHAT'S A punch worth? In boxing, they'll pay boxers a cool million for a fifteen-round heavyweight championship fight. A single punch in a basketball game can cost $3.1 million.

That's what a jury awarded Rudy Tomjanovich, a forward with the Houston Rockets, after he was punched in the face by Kermit Washington of the Los Angeles Lakers, on December 9, 1972. The award—considerably more than the $2.7 million Tomjanovich had asked for—surprised Tomjanovich and stunned the sports world, which had come to accept fisticuffs as part of the game in most major-league activities. The jury, however, remembered the pictures of Tomjanovich's face following the punch. Tomjanovich suffered a skull fracture, a concussion, a broken nose, a separated upper jaw, minor injuries to his eyes, and cuts around the mouth.

The fight—if it could be called that—between Tomjanovich and Washington lasted one punch, and actually started as a duel of elbows between Washington and Rockets' center Kevin Kunnert. Lakers' star Kareem Abdul-Jabbar stepped between the two men and grabbed Washington's left arm. But Washington, 6 feet 8 inches and 250 pounds, still had his right arm free and was able to flatten Kunnert with a punch. Tomjanovich, who had seen the fight across the court, made a run toward Washington, who spun around and let loose another punch. Tomjanovich flew backward, hit his head on the ground, and lay motionless for several minutes before he was helped off the court.

At first Tomjanovich's injuries were not thought to be severe.

Only days later the full extent became clear, and he was ruled out of action for the rest of the season.

The day after the fight Washington said, "I feel bad, really bad, about the whole incident. I couldn't sleep at all last night. I saw him [Tomjanovich] coming at me and I just swung. I had no idea who it was. Now that I've talked to other people, I understand Rudy wasn't going to fight. He's never even been in a fight. It was an honest, unfortunate mistake." Not so, said Rockets' coach Tom Nissalke. "It's the most malicious thing I've ever seen in basketball. It was a damn sucker punch. Washington has no guts. If he's not out for the year, it's a disgrace."

Washington ended up suspended sixty days and fined $10,000 by the National Basketball Association. Besides the fine, Washington also lost an estimated $50,000 in salary, as NBA players cannot be paid while under league suspension.

Tomjanovich underwent numerous operations to rebuild the base structure of his face and plastic surgery to make himself presentable. Meanwhile, the Rockets, who had been expected to contend for their division title, fell to the middle of the pack. -

In October of 1978 Tomjanovich came back to play for the Suns, and league observers felt he was as effective as ever. But was he ever worried he might not make it back? "Yes, I doubted it. I doubted if I would ever walk in public. The way I looked when I got out of the hospital, I wanted to stay in my room and never leave. I didn't believe anyone could look so bad and not be laid out; I mean dead."

In August of 1979 a jury had the final say when it awarded Tomjanovich $3.3 million, later reduced by a judge to the $3.1 million figure. As one columnist summed up the award, "Maybe in sports in this country, money is the only thing that really talks. For that reason alone, I repeat, the Tomjanovich jury is to be commended."

JOHN MATUSZAK

JOHN MATUSZAK is hard to miss; at 6 feet 8 inches, he'd stand out in any crowd. On the football field, he made it to two Super Bowls with the Oakland Raiders. Off the field, he compiled another list of accomplishments, including an acting career and a propensity to find himself in the back of a police squad car.

Here's a partial list of his off-field adventures:

• He transferred from the University of Missouri to Tampa after a scuffle. "I gave a guy a new face," said Matuszak, who also admitted that the incident cost him $80,000.

• In August of 1976 he was charged with possession of four grams of marijuana in Tampa.

• In April of 1982, while back in his home town of Oak Creek, he was arrested for disorderly conduct after a scuffle at the Sawmill Saloon; a month later he was accused of punching a man at Hank's Pub in nearby Milwaukee.

• In July of 1984, a year after he retired from football, Matuszak was arrested after he drove by the scene of an earlier incident involving a friend who kicked a hole in the door of a house. He said he returned to be a good Samaritan. Instead police arrested him for drunken driving and having a 9-mm semiautomatic pistol on the floor of his Lincoln Continental. He was eventually sentenced to five days in jail.

• In January of 1986 he was fined $350 for drunken driving in Milwaukee.

• In June of 1986 Matuszak was ruled innocent of roughing up a male stripper and an emcee at a California bar during a ladies night that turned into a brawl. Matuszak's attorney said the ex-player was targeted because of his celebrity status.

• In June of 1987 Matuszak was sentenced to five days in jail in Los Angeles after he admitted punching a man and attempting to rip the door off his car after a traffic accident.

Matuszak admitted he was often embarrassed by his behavior. "My mom has two scrapbooks. One has all the good things I did in it. One has all the bad things."

KEN PATERA

IN THE wrestling ring, Ken Patera and Mr. Saito were paid good money to participate in team matches. Outside the ring, however, their involvement in a two-man match against the police cost them good time.

Patera—once an Olympic lifter billed as the World's Strongest Man after becoming the first man to lift 500 pounds in a weight-lifting competition—and Saito (whose legal first name was Masanori) were sentenced to two years in prison in 1985 after a fight with police in Waukesha, a suburb of Milwaukee, where they were to wrestle in a professional event.

The police were called to investigate a report that Patera had thrown a thirty-pound rock through a McDonald's restaurant window after being refused service when the restaurant was closed. When two officers arrived at a Holiday Inn to question the pair, a fight began, and the two responding officers, Jacalyn B. Hibbard and John D. Dillon, ended up seriously injured.

Records from a civil lawsuit filed by the officers against the pair said that Hibbard's head was slammed from hallway wall to wall by Patera after he lifted her by her shirt collar and pants' waist. The records went on to say she was knocked unconscious when Saito dropped his knee on the back of her neck.

Hibbard, nineteen at the time, suffered broken teeth, dizzy spells, headaches, a ruptured appendix, and numbness to her face. She ended up retiring from the police force. Dillon suffered a broken leg.

According to a police account of the incident, at one point Saito took up a martial arts stance and fended off officers as he asked repeatedly, "What about my eye?" The report said that one Waukesha officer hit Saito on the back of his leg with a nightstick and that, when Saito turned around, another officer did the same. But, according to reports, while this caught his attention, it did not restrain Saito from coming after the officers. Eventually, thirteen officers were needed to subdue the pair.

In the trial that followed, Patera maintained his innocence, saying he only acted in self-defense after police sprayed his eyes with a chemical. Patera's lawyer also showed video tapes of a Patera match, instructing jurors not to confuse his clients' bad-guy persona in the ring with that of his real-life demeanor. The jury, however, did not agree with the wrestlers, and a judge sentenced the pair, with an admonition that they were lucky no one was killed in the incident.

While Saito was a model prisoner, according to officials, Patera continued to claim his innocence. "There's no reason for Saito and me to be in prison," he said to a reporter. "I feel very strongly that I don't owe a debt to society, because I was provoked into protecting myself. I'll die with that conviction."

Both wrestlers were released from prison after serving eighteen months, and both said they were going to return to wrestling careers.

WOODY HAYES

HUGH HINDMAN will probably go down in sports history as the answer to a trivia question—that is, who fired Woody Hayes?

"It's true," said Hindman in 1979. "People will probably remember me as the man who fired Woody. But if I had my way, I'd rather be remembered as the man who hired Earle Bruce."

Here's the next question: Who did Hayes hit to force Hindman to fire him?

It was middle guard Charlie Bauman of Clemson, who intercepted a pass with two minutes remaining in the 1978 Gator Bowl in Jacksonville, Florida. Bauman aroused Hayes's wrath with his interception, which probably wiped out any chance Ohio State had to overcome a 17–15 deficit, the margin by which the team eventually lost.

After Bauman picked off the pass thrown by Ohio State quarterback Art Schlichter (See Schlichter's own entry in "Abuse"), Bauman was forced out of bounds in front of the Ohio State bench.

In front of a national television audience, Bauman then waved the ball in Hayes's face and taunted him. Hayes retaliated by punching Bauman. Television cameras then caught Hayes punching one of his own players in the confusion that followed. The player, guard Ken Fritz, was trying to restrain Hayes.

After ten minutes of a bench-clearing brawl, Hayes was hit with a fifteen-yard penalty for unsportsmanlike conduct, then another fifteen yarder for yelling at officials on the next play.

But the next morning, Hayes was given the ultimate penalty—he was fired, at about the same time he was telling a newsman he had quit.

So ended a career in which Hayes, called by some one of the greatest college football coaches ever, recorded 238 victories, 72 defeats, and 10 ties, and won or shared 13 Big Ten conference titles.

Hayes's accomplishments, however, were clouded by his hair-trigger temper. In 1973 Hayes shoved the camera of a *Los Angeles Times* photographer into the journalist's face as he took photographs during a Rose Bowl pregame period. The photographer required treatment for minor injuries. In 1974 Hayes belted a Michigan State fan minutes after the Spartans upset Hayes's previously unbeaten team, 16–13, in East Lansing. In 1977 Hayes was placed on probation by the Big Ten after he took a swing at an ABC cameraman on the sideline. It was actually Hayes's second probationary period; in 1956 he was found to have been advancing players personal money.

Yet in 1987, when Hayes died in his sleep at age seventy-four, he was remembered as a "caring person." "What sticks out in my mind right now are all the good things he did for his former players and coaches," said Earle Bruce, the assistant who eventually replaced Hayes. "He always had a lot of time for them. He was a tremendously different person off the field than on. Off the field, he knew everybody's name and always had a word of advice. On the field, he was quite demanding, to say the least."

FIGHTING WORDS

"We've got to mold a lineup that can take on a bunch of goons. I'm looking for guys you toss raw meat to and they go wild."
—Harold Ballard, Toronto Maple Leafs' president

"If they took away our sticks, and gave us brooms, we'd still have fights."
—Phil Esposito, New York Rangers

SOCCER RIOTS TO REMEMBER

These were some of the worst soccer riots in history:
• Lima, Peru. May 24, 1964. 318 killed, 500 injured.
An Olympic qualifying match between Peru and Argentina turned ugly when, with two minutes to play, a Peruvian goal was disallowed because of a referee's call. Peruvian fans ran onto the field and attacked the referee; security officials responded with tear gas and live bullets. Most of those killed were spectators who stampeded into a locked stadium gate while trying to escape.

• Buenos Aires, Argentina. June 23, 1968. 73 dead, 200 injured.
A group of young ruffians began a riot by throwing burning

paper into the crowd during a match between River and the Boca Juniors, causing a stampede.

• Brussels, Belgium. May 1985. 42 killed, 400 injured.
In the most far-reaching incident recorded, English fans present at the European Cup finals game attacked fans of an Italian team. Afterward, English teams were barred from international play.

Billy Martin

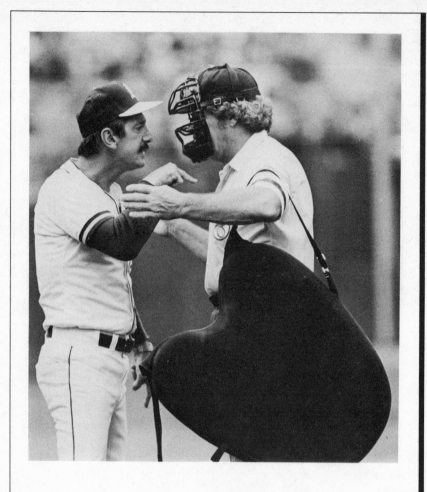

Billy Martin argues with home-plate umpire Terry Cooney during a 1982 game at the Oakland Coliseum. (AP/Wide World Photos)

Can you ever protest too much? Martin and centerfielder
Dwayne Murphy were both thumbed from this game—Oakland
As versus the Detroit Tigers. (AP/Wide World Photos)

In a picture taken from a television monitor, Kermit Washington
is shown just after punching Rudy Tomjanovich in the face.
(AP/Wide World Photos)

Rudy Tomjanovich

John Matuszak works out to stay in fighting shape. (Milwaukee Journal)

FLAKES

MARK FIDRYCH

BILL LEE

JOE DON LOONEY

JOHN RIGGINS

JOHNNY LOGAN

There are some athletes whose mental capacities have been, well, lower than their batting averages or shooting percentages. Many of these characters, however, have been truly lovable.

MARK FIDRYCH

THEY CALLED him "the Bird" because he looked like the character Big Bird on "Sesame Street." Mark Fidrych had a gangly walk, curly hair, and an ever-present smile, and when they handed him the ball and he strode out to the pitcher's mound, it was pure magic.

Fidrych pitched his way to rookie of the year honors with the Detroit Tigers, and he did it with style. On the mound, Fidrych was a one-man show. If he didn't like the feel of the dirt around the mound's rubber, he had no qualms about getting down on his knees to pat each and every grain into place, and before pitches he would talk to the ball, telling it just where he wanted it to go.

During his first season the ball often went where the Massachusetts native wanted it to. He had a 19–9 record, led the American League in earned run average with a 2.34 figure, was the starting pitcher for the league in the All-Star game, and was then named the league's top rookie.

He pumped life into the Tiger organization and the entire league, and his twenty-nine starts that season, at home and away, drew more than 900,000 fans.

The owner of a bar next to Tiger Stadium said, "The place hasn't been like this since we won the 1968 Series."

Rusty Staub, a Detroit teammate, said, "Every person can see the enthusiasm in Mark. He brings out the exuberance and inner youth in everybody."

A season later, however, the Bird's wings were clipped—forever as it turned out. In spring training that 1977 season, Fidrych suffered a knee injury. Later that season he began experiencing shoulder problems.

The next four seasons were a roller coaster, from the majors to the minors and back, with time on the disabled list. He pitched in just twenty-seven games in all from 1977 to 1980. Finally he was released by the Tigers after the 1981 season, which he spent in the minors.

The Boston Red Sox, managed by Ralph Houk, Fidrych's manager at Detroit in 1976 and 1977, gave him another chance. But in June of 1983, with a 2–5 record and 9.68 ERA, he was told by his minor-league manager that the team needed a spot on the roster for another pitcher. Realizing they meant his spot, Fidrych, at twenty-eight, retired, rather than have the club release him.

He returned to a farm in Northboro, Massachusetts, where he mused on his amazing story. He said the years of torturous rehabilitation he endured were worth it. "I wanted to play baseball. I wanted to play in the big leagues," he said. "I had that fever. I had the taste. It was like giving a piece of candy to a baby. Give him one piece, he wants another piece. Well, I got four and a half years of that candy, and that life up there is great."

He added that he didn't feel cheated by the injuries that ended his career. "I had ten great years of baseball, no matter if it was the minor leagues or the major leagues," Fidrych said. "I got ten years out of my life where I got to do what I wanted to do, play baseball. If you think you got cheated, all you do is look back at your friends that you played ball with that never even saw a major-league uniform."

BILL LEE

BILL LEE earned the nickname "Spaceman" for the supposed holes in his head. Was it really Lee who was the airhead? In a sport with all the originality of an auto production line, where ballplayers talk of ERAs and RBIs as if they were of earth-shattering importance, Lee was a breath of fresh air.

About busing in Boston he said, "Maybe busing isn't the answer, but try it at least. People got to live together." He called then Yankee manager Billy Martin, "A neo Nazi." His contribution toward zero population was: "Order a two-year moratorium on births. But then Johnson and Johnson and the diaper companies would get after me."

Lee entered baseball in 1969. He won seventeen games a season for three straight years, from 1973–1975, and about the same time started drawing national attention for his unusual behavior.

Writers found him to be great copy. Throw out a few straight lines and a couple of serious topics, and Lee's mouth was off to the races. An instant article was born.

But if Lee was a media favorite, his team—the stodgy Boston Red Sox—was less than thrilled, especially after Lee's record took a dive in the 1976 season.

In September 1977 the *Washington Post* wrote, "The charm of Lee seems to have worn thin here. You can't be a human being and play big league baseball at the same time. . . . Lee refuses to believe it. He believes you can love your family, care about society, and rejoice in the company of friends—and still play baseball well."

If the Red Sox needed an excuse to get rid of Lee, it came in June of 1978, when he staged a one-day walkout and called the Red Sox management "gutless" for the sale of his friend and teammate Bernie Carbo.

Dealt to the Montreal Expos before the 1979 season, he turned in a 16–10 performance in a season that included more controversy.

While being interviewed by a newspaper reporter about reports of drug use on the Red Sox, he was asked if he used marijuana. He replied, "Certainly, I use it. I've used it since 1968. I never brought it to the ball park, but I've used it since then, personally." Oops. A member of the baseball commissioner's security staff was sent immediately to interview Lee, who changed his story a bit, saying, "I never used the stuff." That satisfied the lords of baseball, and the issue was dropped.

Lee's statistics slipped again the next two seasons, and by 1982 he had worn out his welcome in Montreal.

The final incident was another dispute with management over the release of a friend. This time the Expos had released second baseman Rodney Scott. In an action similar to his Boston boycott, Lee left the stadium before a scheduled game, ripping his uniform off and throwing it on a stool.

"I was furious when I found out about Rodney," Lee said later.

Lee left the team an address: Brasserie 77, a Montreal tavern. Sure enough, he returned during the game, three pints of beer heavier.

After the game, the Expos released the thirty-five-year-old Lee, saying, "We'd been thinking about it for some time." Lee signed his release form: "Bill Lee, Earth '82."

Lee tried a comeback in 1987 but left the minor-league team during the season after a dispute with management.

JOE DON LOONEY

OTTO GRAHAM, one of the most respected names in football's history, said that Joe Don Looney could have been one of the National Football League's greatest fullbacks. Instead, Looney will probably go down as one of the league's biggest disappointments and one of its greatest flakes.

Looney's troubles started in the early 1960s, when Oklahoma University coach Bud Wilkinson decided he couldn't handle the 6-foot 1-inch, 200-pound All-American, and he was dropped from the squad.

He went on to the NFL, and after he became a first-round draft choice of the New York Giants in 1964, his career record reads like a "Where's Where" of the NFL. It started when the Giants traded him to the Baltimore Colts later in 1964. Then he was traded by the Colts to the Detroit Lions in 1965, and traded by the Lions to the Washington Redskins in 1966.

Looney left a wake of trauma instead of stellar statistics.

In New York he was late for meals, missed team buses, and refused to deal with the press. He was fined more than all of his teammates combined but accepted the penalties politely and cheerfully.

In Baltimore he and a friend smashed in an apartment door and assaulted the owner. He explained, "I'd been sitting on the bench all year and Goldwater had just lost the election. I had to take it out on somebody."

In Detroit he was fined $250 for brawling in a restaurant near training camp and then skipping practice. The Lions finally gave up on him when he refused to return to a game in which he was being used to relay plays, saying, "If you want a messenger, call Western Union."

Dropped by the Redskins in 1967, he married, went to Vietnam for nine months, came back, and tried football again with the New Orleans Saints but was injured and forced to retire. He was also divorced.

Looney next showed up in 1977 in Ganeshpur, India, at what one writer called "a spiritual training camp" for the Swami Baba Muktananda. Looney said that he joined the Swami in 1975 after his experiences in Vietnam. "I saw a guy die and said, 'To hell with it.' I'm not ever going to jump through the hoop for anybody."

His duties in India included tending an elephant, Vijay, for the guru, who said, "Joe and Vijay are very much alike; they are like brothers. When Joe was younger and got angry he used to elbow people like this and that. Vijay does the same thing. I felt they would be great friends."

In 1983 Looney surfaced again, still following his personal guru. In a story in the *Atlanta Journal,* Looney stated that he had been around the world twice in the previous fifteen years. The article said, "Much of his time was spent in India, where he worked as a food buyer, a bodyguard, a laborer, garden keeper, and elephant boy. Eventually, he worked his way up to chief of compost. He claims the world record for shoveling elephant compost—twelve loads in one hour ten minutes, shattering the old mark by two full minutes."

Looney contrasted his life with the Swami with his previous football days, saying, "I like the disciplined life. I like eating regular meals. Everything here is taken care of. The place is clean. The food is on time. It's a matter of getting free. Sure, I like the wind in my face. Athletes are spontaneous people. I don't know what it's like now with all the bucks and the popularity contests, but I did it because I loved to cut loose. That was my payoff."

In September of 1988, at the age of forty-five, Joe Don Looney died—the victim of a tragic motorcycle accident.

JOHN RIGGINS

THERE ARE no pictures to prove it, but John Riggins fell asleep on the floor at an exclusive Washington, D.C., dinner, where Vice President George Bush and members of Congress were giving speeches.

Riggins attended the 1985 Washington Press Club's annual salute to Congress and was seated at a table with Supreme Court Justice Sandra O'Connor. Several times, Riggins—who had been drinking at a cocktail hour—called out to O'Connor, "Come on Sandy baby, loosen up. You're too tight." Later, others at the table said Riggins left his chair, walked around the table, knelt down, sat down, then lay down and fell asleep.

One witness said Riggins slept for about an hour between tables, first on his back, then on his stomach, occasionally snoring as waiters and waitresses served dessert and cleared tables around him. According to another witness, Riggins's head fell near the feet of actor Hugh O'Brian, who told people in a courteous way to "let the guy sleep." After the dinner, guests woke Riggins, who left on his own.

Months after the incident, Riggins was stopped by police near his home in Fairfax County and charged with being drunk in public.

In a rare interview following the two incidents, he said he was "a bad boy" and was embarrassed, and he promised there would be no more such incidents.

More than just a few people winked at that statement. For the

John Riggins they knew had always been, as one teammate put it, someone who "plays to the tune of a different drummer."

There was the time that, as a member of the New York Jets, he cut his hair in a Mohawk. He once showed up at a Super Bowl press conference wearing a T-shirt and camouflage pants, and another time he attended a casual barbecue in tails and a top hat.

Joe Theismann, once Riggins's teammate on the Washington Redskins, said, "John is a real character." "Character" may be an understatement. He's been called perverse by one Washington writer, a chauvinist by another. He's been called independent, alienated, and a malingerer. Television sportscaster Mike Adamle once blurted out that Riggins was "crazy," to which Redskins' owner Jack Kent Cooke responded, "He's not crazy." Riggins has, during the rare times he's talked to the press, said, "I don't think anyone can tell me how to carry a football. No one can tell me how to run my life, either. I figure it's OK as long as I don't go against John Law."

His most memorable moment on the field in pro football came in Super Bowl XVII. With a fourth-down and one-yard situation on the Miami Dolphin forty-three-yard line, Riggins took the ball, found an open spot, bulled through, passed a Miami defender, and ran forty-three yards for a touchdown, to give the Redskins a 20–17 lead, as the Redskins went on to win, 27–17.

Riggins's career ended in March of 1986 when the Redskins released him at the age of thirty-six. He had become the fourth-leading rusher in NFL history with 11,352 yards in fourteen seasons, nine with the Redskins.

JOHNNY LOGAN

Casey Stengel and Yogi Berra were hardly masters of the English language, but the classic lines of at least one baseball all-star may not have made it outside his baseball home town.

These verbal gems came from Johnny Logan, shortstop for the Milwaukee Braves during their glory days in the beer city. When it came to matching quips with Stengel and Berra, Logan was able to hold his own.

- Asked to pick the No. 1 baseball player of all time: "I'd have to go with the immoral Babe Ruth."
- When ordering dessert: "I'll have pie à la mode with ice cream."
- After seeing the play *Macbeth* on television: "They've got this new Shakespearean play, *McBride*. It's got a lot of suspension."
- During a Braves' slump: "We're just tiresome, that's all."
- When he received an award: "I will perish this trophy forever."
- Upon being introduced to someone: "I know the name, but I can't replace the face."
- Discussing the Braves after being traded to Pittsburgh: "They're all right, but they've got too many young youths."
- When the skies darkened and a storm seemed imminent: "It looks like a toronto."

If the mound didn't feel quite right, Fidrych would get down on his knees and do some construction. (Milwaukee Journal)

Mark Fidrych gives special instructions to the ball before pitch-ing. (AP/Wide World Photos)

Bill Lee

Joe Don Looney in his playing days

Training to another tune—former NFL running back Joe Don Looney—a follower of Swami Muktananda (AP/Wide World Photos)

John Riggins

Johnny Logan

SEXUAL CAPERS

TENNIS MATCHES

MARLA COLLINS

MORGANNA

LANCE RENTZEL

JAN STEPHENSON

THE GREAT WIFE SWAP

MICKEY MANTLE

PETE ROSE

KEN STABLER

AWFULLY CUTE COUPLES

In the golden age of sports some half a century ago, athletes often enjoyed a "no-tell" policy when it came to their personal lives. But today divorces, spats, and any sort of affair are all fair game for a probing media.

TENNIS MATCHES

ONE TENNIS pro called it a "gay witch hunt," when reporters from several continents descended like vultures on the women's tour in the spring of 1981.

The *New York Post* wrote, "Lesbian Scandal Shaking Women's Tennis."

Not to be outdone, the *National Enquirer* reportedly offered players on the women's tour as much as $5,000 to talk about lesbianism.

A simple lawsuit, which would end up being dismissed a year later, set off this furor. The object of the suit was no less than Billie Jean King, the matriarch of women's tennis, who was being sued by her former secretary for palimony. Marilyn Barnett claimed that she had lived with—and loved—King in an affair that began in 1972.

At first, King denied the report. But only days later, with her husband Larry at her side, she admitted that she did have an affair with Barnett. Saying that Barnett had become "unstable," King called the liaison "a mistake." She added, "I will assume the responsibility. I discussed it with Larry. In some ways, I think we're much closer today than we've ever been, and our marriage is stronger."

Women's tennis hadn't suffered its last tremor of the year. Only months later Martina Navratilova, one of King's successors as queen of tennis, admitted she too had a female lover.

There had long been rumors surrounding Navratilova, a Czechoslovakian defector who later gained American citizenship, particularly since she was a close friend of lesbian activist and author Rita Mae Brown.

But it wasn't confirmed until the *New York Post,* in a copyrighted story in July of 1981, wrote that Navratilova had admitted to having bisexual affairs but was afraid to talk about them publicly because she was worried that corporate sponsors would drop women's tennis.

What was the big deal? Hadn't athletes—both men and women—previously admitted gay and bisexual affairs? Indeed they had. But King and Navratilova, two of tennis's most popular figures, and both still active as players and organizers, were coming out of the closet.

Navratilova, in her autobiography entitled *Martina,* wrote, "It really shouldn't matter that much, but I am told that image counts a lot in the world. Advertisers and sponsors pay a lot of money because of image. At the time of the Billie Jean revelations, there was concern about Avon dropping sponsorships if they felt there was too much bad publicity. They denied they were getting out—but they were gone within a year."

Unlike King, Navratilova never apologized for her relationship with Brown. She wrote, "The months with Rita Mae formed one of those romantic times. We started traveling together—long dinners, and glasses of wine, suede and lace and silk instead of Gatorade and warm-up suits—and I got to know her better."

Despite Navratilova's concerns, women's tennis survived. Both King and Navratilova found their careers anything but damaged. And in 1982 a California judge dismissed the palimony suit against King, saying that Barnett had no grounds on which to pursue it. Days earlier King had been named on the World Almanac's list of most influential women in the United States, finishing third behind Supreme Court Justice Sandra O'Connor and *Washington Post* chairman Katharine Graham.

Navratilova went on to rewrite the tennis record books. With the help of basketball star Nancy Lieberman she rose to the number-one spot in the world. The two held a press conference to say they were going to live together but that Lieberman was straight. "If two gays lived together, nobody thinks anything. If two guys live together, they don't either. We have one gay and one straight, what's the big deal?" said Navratilova.

Along with Navratilova's success came riches. One sports columnist nicknamed her "Miss Moneybags," for among her sponsorship deals was a contract for a reported $2.5 million to wear and promote Puma shoes for five years. "She is perhaps the most marketable woman in sports," said one agent.

MARLA COLLINS

MARLA COLLINS wore two uniforms in her *Playboy* layout in 1986. The first was regulation Chicago Cubs, the same uniform she wore as a ball girl for the team. The second was all Marla. When the Cubs' management saw her new outfit they thumbed her out, and stripped her of the Cubs' pinstripes.

The ensuing controversy made good print for Chicago newspapers and better gossip for talk shows. It undoubtedly sold a lot of issues of *Playboy,* as Cubs' fans scurried to see their Marla modeling an outfit that conveniently left nothing to the imagination.

How she and the Cubs ended up separating depends on who you believe. The Cubs admitted calling Collins into the office, and the team then issued a statement in which it was said the two sides parted amicably: "Marla Collins has left the Chicago Cubs organization effective today. The organization has not made a decision regarding a replacement for Marla." Collins said that she was fired.

At least one Chicago sports columnist threw a few barbs at the Cubs, saying, "Until Tuesday Collins worked for the Cubs at Wrigley Field. Her job was to hand baseballs to the umpire, a function of approximately the skill level of celery. She wore very short pants and did her own makeup. She nearly never missed an opportunity to bend over. The Cubs did not discourage her from showing her legs and smiling at customers who leered at her. That is why she was there."

Collins said that when she posed for the pictures, she was told the layout would come out after the baseball season was over. Her agent said, however, that Collins was not planning to return to the Cubs the following season anyway, as she was going to be married in the fall. Her agent added, "Everybody knew getting fired was a distinct possibility the minute we entered into the project. Despite that, we decided to go on with it. The main reason is she can't see herself being a ball girl forever. It was financially rewarding. Otherwise we wouldn't have done it."

For a time, at least, Collins, who said that she thinks she received around $25,000 for the layout, was a celebrity. She was hired by organizations, including at least one minor-league baseball team, to appear at their functions.

At a Muskies baseball game in Madison, she told a newspaper reporter that she hoped the *Playboy* exposure would advance her career. She said that she wanted to be on the radio, try modeling, and, after that, open a boutique, "maybe lingerie."

Collins also admitted that the text accompanying the pictures was a bit exaggerated. One caption said, "At game's end she leaves Wrigley and goes home to put on something more comfortable." In the pictures, "more comfortable" meant off with her uniform top and shorty shorts and on with a black lace jacket, garter belt, and stockings, all sequined in gold. The finishing touch was stiletto-heeled pumps. Collins giggled and said, "Comfortable. When I want to be comfortable I go home and put on a sweatsuit. Or pajamas."

She took issue with the Cubs' management, saying it was hypocritical, because if they had not wanted a ball retriever who doubled as a sex symbol, "why didn't they just have a boy do it? They were the ones that kept getting me to cut off my shorts shorter and shorter," she said.

Marla would probably have had a lot of sympathy from a group of Dallas Cowboy cheerleaders who, in 1978, found themselves the object of a hot poster but ended up resigning en masse because of what they termed "ridiculous rules" enforced by the club. They then posed for a similar poster—this time with blouses open and breasts exposed.

MORGANNA

SHE HAS her own baseball cards, her own nickname, and her own major-league statistics. She's Morganna, better known as the "Kissing Bandit." She made herself a household name in the late 1970s and early 1980s by running onto baseball fields during games to plant kisses on the cheeks of unsuspecting players.

It was a hobby that started in 1970 as a result of a dare. It didn't end until she had bounced her way onto the pages of *Playboy* magazine. Why *Playboy*? Let's check the back of her baseball cards for those vital statistics: 60–24–39. As *Playboy* put it, she had "the biggest bust ever featured in an exclusive *Playboy* pictorial." And the magazine added, "It should retain that title as long as gravity holds sway over human hydraulics."

The term "gravity" often seemed to be mentioned in the same breath as Morganna's name. There was the time in Houston when she was jailed and tried for her on-the-field antics. "My lawyer used the 'law-of-gravity defense,'" she said. The lawyer argued that Morganna was sitting in a front-row box and leaned over to scoop up a foul ground ball, toppling onto the field in the process. The judge dismissed the charges.

A baseball fan since her youth in Kentucky, Morganna said she started her routine in 1970 during a Cincinnati Reds' game when she ran onto the field to kiss Pete Rose. "A girlfriend dirty-double-dared me to do it," Morganna said. "Where I'm from, you don't turn down a dirty-double-dare . . . at least, not when you're a teenager."

Rose's reaction was less than approving. "He used terrible language," she said. "The next night, however, he tracked me down to the local nightspot where I was appearing and apologized with a bunch of roses."

Later, as she began a nightclub routine, she added more "victims." Nolan Ryan, Steve Yeager, George Brett, Mike Schmidt, Steve Garvey, Mark (the Bird) Fidrych, and even the San Diego Chicken were hit by the kissing bandit. "I always kiss them on the cheek," she said. "It's more sanitary than the lips, and that way their wives don't get upset."

While her usual on-the-field uniform consisted of a tight top stretched to its fullest and short shorts, her *Playboy* layout in June of 1983 consisted of a little pink lingerie top that could hardly cover everything. And in several shots in her bathtub, there was even less.

In 1986 Morganna took her love of the game one step further, buying a limited partnership in the Utica Blue Sox minor league baseball team. And yes, she showed up that year at the park to kiss some players.

LANCE RENTZEL

THE UNION of Joey Heatherton, the quintessential cheerleader, and Lance Rentzel, the ultimate fair-haired and handsome football hero, looked like a marriage made in heaven, "or perhaps in the mind of some writer of scenarios for a 1930s college musical," said a newspaper article in 1970.

One month later Rentzel's hero's image was shattered when he was arrested for exposing himself to a ten-year-old girl. Less than a year later dancer/actress Heatherton was filing for divorce, citing irreconcilable differences.

By then, the praise Rentzel received all his life had turned to humiliation. He wrote about himself that, "Lance Rentzel found the secret to success: plenty of exposure. . . . Rentzel will never be convicted because the evidence will not stand up in court. . . . Rentzel is hoping for a hung jury."

Rentzel's arrest came during his fourth season with the Dallas Cowboys of the National Football League, a career during which he became "one of the top flankers in the league," according to coach Tom Landry. But Landry made that statement only when he was ridding himself of Rentzel, in May of 1971, when the team traded Rentzel to the Los Angeles Rams for tight end Billy Truax and wide receiver Wendell Tucker.

Rentzel said that he welcomed the trade. "When you think about it, I think this is the best thing for all parties. I'm grateful they traded me to an area where I have so many friends and to such a good team and a fine organization. But I still owe a debt to Dallas for standing behind me."

The Cowboys were among the few that did stand behind Rentzel after his arrest in late November of 1970 in University Park, a suburb of Dallas. The police report said that Rentzel, who was twenty-seven at the time, drove up to the girl in his car, talked to her, exposed himself, then drove away. Rentzel pleaded guilty to the charge and was given five-years probation, providing he received medical and psychiatric care.

At the time of the arrest, it was revealed that Rentzel had entered a guilty plea in 1966 in a similar case in St. Paul while he was playing with the Minnesota Vikings, who had picked him in the second round of the 1965 draft from the University of Oklahoma.

Rentzel's problems with the law didn't end with his trade to the Rams. In 1973 he was sentenced to ninety days in jail and fined $2,000 for possession of marijuana after a search of his Hollywood apartment.

The NFL, which had previously only put Rentzel on probation, then suspended him indefinitely "for conduct detrimental to the NFL." After sitting out the entire 1973 season, Rentzel was reinstated for the 1974 season but caught only eighteen passes that season and scored only one touchdown, down from his 1969 total of forty-three receptions and twelve touchdowns. The Rams released Rentzel before the 1975 season.

In his 1972 autobiography *When All the Laughter Died in Sorrow,* Rentzel described the origins of his problems and his struggles to overcome them. He admitted that he was not helped at all by those who defended him—including his parents, his college football coach Bud Wilkinson, and others who could not believe Lance Rentzel would ever do such a thing.

He also described the University Park incident. ". . . I found myself pulling over to the curb in front of a big house with a spacious lawn. I was only a few blocks from my apartment, but I didn't realize it. In fact, I didn't seem to know or care where I was or what I was doing, but I was drawn by the sight of a young girl playing in the front yard. All reason, all judgment, all foresight were momentarily suspended in my mind. It suddenly seemed that through that girl, some vital reassurance would come to me. I called her to the car as though to ask a question, exposed myself, and drove away. The rest of the day passed by like a dream. . . ."

Little has been heard from Rentzel since his retirement from pro football.

JAN STEPHENSON

SUPERSTAR GOLFER Jan Stephenson found it wasn't so easy being a sex symbol. Waiting for the photographer to set up his camera while she was lying in a bathtub, seemingly in the nude and covered only by golf balls, she didn't expect that particular picture to turn up in a calendar.

"Good gosh," Jan said. "I figured they were going to turn out a regular calendar. I just arrived in all my clothes, golf clothes. But by the end of the day, most of my clothes were off." What's a girl to do?

The revealing photos were used in a 1986 calendar by the Dunlop Company. One picture was the famous Jan-in-the-tub-with-golf-balls shot. But was Jan—who once said she turned down $50,000 to pose nude for *Playboy*—really in her birthday suit? No, she said later, she was actually wearing a bikini. And she added that the session was no picnic. "The balls were very heavy and it was very uncomfortable," she added.

How did Jan like the calendar? "When I saw the calendar, I said, 'Surely this is a joke.' I couldn't believe it. What happened to all the pictures with my clothes on?"

Nice try, Jan. One would have thought that by 1986 Stephenson would have been used to seeing most of her body displayed in pictures. It was Stephenson, after all, who appeared in 1977 on the cover of *Sport Magazine* wearing a blouse that showed off her ample chest. And in 1981 she was part of a controversial picture spread in *Fairway Magazine,* the official publication of the Ladies Professional Golf Association, where in one picture she was resting on a bed, in a slinky white dress, revealing lots and lots of thigh.

"Quasi-pornography" cried one of Stephenson's fellow golfers, Jane Blalock. "Is our organization so unaware of the real glamor and attraction staring it in the face that it must resort to such trash?" Other pros came to Stephenson's defense. JoAnne Carner, a U.S. Open winner, said, "If I had legs like Jan, I would pose like that, too."

The exposure didn't seem to hurt Stephenson's game or the outside attention she received. She was named one of the ten most watchable women in 1978, along with such beauties as Sophia Loren, Phyllis George, and Cheryl Tiegs.

In 1983 she recorded her best season ever on the LPGA circuit, winning one tournament and finishing fourth on the money-earnings list with $193,364. It's tough being a sex symbol.

THE GREAT WIFE SWAP

QUICK, WHAT'S baseball's most memorable trade? Norm Cash for Steve Demeter? Orlando Cepeda for Ray Sadecki? Many would look back to the spring of 1973 at what became known as the "great wife swap."

It all started when the New York Yankees announced that two of the team's pitchers, Mike Kekich and Fritz Peterson, had swapped wives and families the previous year. Kekich's wife, Susanne, and two daughters, aged four and two, moved in with Peterson, while Peterson's wife, Marilyn—whose nickname was Chip—and two sons, aged six and two, moved in with Kekich. "There was nothing dirty about it," Peterson said at the time. "This was not a wife swap, it was a life swap."

How did the deal turn out? It was not, as they say in baseball, a trade that helped both clubs. After a few months Marilyn moved out on Kekich, while Peterson and Kekich's wife stayed together. Kekich was left "out in the cold," as he put it.

Meanwhile Peterson talked about how the whole thing began. "We've known each other for three or four years. In the beginning it was fun just being together, the four of us. Then, as things went along, it became more serious. It all started last July 15. We were living in Franklin Lakes, and Mike and Susanne were living in Mahwah [about eight miles away]. Mike started to campaign for my wife about in August. He talked to me seriously about it. He told his own wife that he loved Marilyn more. That started it. Marilyn didn't think he was serious at first. She thought it was funny at first, and so did I. Then we all discussed it seriously and we agreed."

The Yankees' official response was noncommital at first. Ralph Houk, the team's field manager, said, "It doesn't bother me other than what effect it might have on their pitching. Their personal lives are their own business. The two players were asked if it would be better if one of them was traded, but neither of them indicated it would affect their feeling on the field or in the clubhouse."

But 1973 ended up being the pair's last year with the Yankees. Kekich was traded in midseason to the Cleveland Indians—"Obviously, they kept the consistent winner, Fritz," Kekich said—but was let go by the Indians a week before the 1974 season. Unconfirmed reports said that Kekich was dumped because the Yankees wanted to trade Peterson to the Indians, who were not interested in keeping them both.

While pitching for the Indians, Kekich suffered what he called a "nervous breakdown." "I walked to the mound in Milwaukee when it happened," he said later. "I went dizzy. My vision was foggy, yet I wasn't physically ill. I couldn't believe what was happening to me. I always held emotions and jitters well inside me. It seemed like my whole body was going to burst. My muscles felt like solid bone."

Kekich was able to pitch the game but was not able to last until his next assignment. After the Indians gave up on Kekich, he signed with the Texas Rangers and was sent to the team's Triple A farm club in Spokane, but said he couldn't afford it, and went to play in Japan.

In 1975 he rejoined the Rangers but appeared in only twenty-three games and did not record a win or loss. He was released in the spring of 1976. In 1977, picked up by the Seattle Mariners, Kekich said, "It's been a long time since I've been happy. If someone wanted to make a graph to illustrate my life and my career since 1973, it would look like a mountain range."

Peterson's career went much more smoothly immediately following the announcement, but it didn't last much longer. After almost two full seasons with the Indians, he was traded to the Texas Rangers in 1976 and given his release by the Rangers that same season.

Neither Kekich nor Peterson had much to say in later years

about the swap. In fact, Kekich said, "We have had all the publicity we want in our personal lives. I'm not sorry for anything I did. Nor is Marilyn. Our side of the story has never been told, and it never will be. I've been offered $100,000 for it by a publisher. [The] children on both sides have been hurt enough."

After his career ended, Peterson moved to Barrington, a Chicago suburb, and Susanne Peterson was contacted there in 1977. She refused to discuss anything about their lives, except to say she and her husband were involved in Christian work. "We met some wonderful Christian people and decided that was the only way to live."

MICKEY MANTLE

MICKEY MANTLE is one of the legendary figures in sports history. That's why, when Jim Bouton wrote about him in less-than-reverent terms in his *Ball Four* exposé, Bouton incurred the wrath of a Mantle-adoring sports public. "Nothing in *Ball Four* attracted as much noisy reaction as the few remarks I wrote about the man who has become a kind of American folk hero," wrote Bouton in a followup book.

What had Bouton said? He didn't accuse Mantle of any crime, just a bit of extra-hours activity. Bouton used the term *beaver shooting*. Baseball players, he went on to say, took to scientific extremes the art of seeking out women in various stages of undress—or from very compromising angles.

Some players used to hang from fire escapes; others would chin themselves on transoms. Still others would drill holes in the back of a dugout, hoping to get a glimpse of the tender areas of an unsuspecting female fan. And Bouton wrote that Mantle—the mighty Mick—was right in there with the best of them.

A certain hotel, Bouton wrote, provided the Yankees of the 1960s with beaver shooting opportunities as "a series of L-shaped wings . . . made windows particularly vulnerable from certain spots on the roof."

Bouton, a member of the team, said some expeditions were led by none other than Mantle himself. In squads of fifteen or so, players would head to the roofs and spread out. When a victim was spotted, they would whistle and call out a room number so all could view.

Bouton wrote about the reaction to *Ball Four* in another book, *I'm Glad You Didn't Take It Personally,* where he recounted some of the backlash from his first book, which has since been called one of the classics of sports literature. Mantle, Bouton stated, was held high as the "perfect hero." He went on to say that to the public, Mantle seemed all but perfect and that no one—or almost no one—wanted to know anything different.

Mantle himself was said to have replied only once to a question of what he thought of Jim Bouton's book, "Jim who?"

PETE ROSE

"When I first got married, I worried about the groupies; then I said to myself, 'Karolyn, he's got to find someone much better, and that ain't gonna be easy.' "—Karolyn Rose, wife of baseball player Pete Rose, in the spring of 1974

In April of 1984 Rose, now with the Montreal Expos, showed up in Montreal with his new wife, Carol, after their marriage that day. In October the Roses had a baby and named him Tyler Edward Rose (Ty was the nickname of the man whose hitting total Rose chased). Rose and his previous wife, Karolyn, were divorced in August of 1980, only months after Rose settled a paternity suit with a Tampa woman out of court.

KEN STABLER

"One night I was in bed with a girl there. The stereo was on and I didn't hear anyone enter the house. Wanda had not only slipped in, she had come into the bedroom behind me. She didn't say a word. She just picked up a metal trash can and cracked me in the back of the head. Quarterback interruptus! For a full minute my head was filled with those black stars you see when a flashbulb goes off in your eyes.

"I jumped up naked, grabbed my clothes, and locked myself in the bathroom while I got dressed. . . ."
—Ken Stabler, from his book *Snake*

AWFULLY CUTE COUPLES

MAMIE VAN DOREN AND BO BELINSKY
NORM NIXON AND DEBBIE ALLEN (of "Fame" fame)
AHMAD RASHAD AND PHYLICIA AYERS-ALLEN
DEAN PAUL MARTIN AND DOROTHY HAMILL
TOMMY MASON AND CATHY RIGBY
JIMMY CONNORS AND CHRIS EVERT
JIMMY CONNORS AND PATTI McGUIRE
CHRIS EVERT AND BURT REYNOLDS
CHRIS EVERT AND JOHN LLOYD
JOHN McENROE AND TATUM O'NEAL
VITAS GERULAITIS AND JANET JONES
FRANK GIFFORD AND KATHIE LEE JOHNSON
JOE THEISMANN AND CATHY LEE CROSBY
JOJO STARBUCK AND TERRY BRADSHAW
RAY KNIGHT AND NANCY LOPEZ
BRUCE JENNER AND CHRISTIE
JOE NAMATH AND SUZY STORM
JOE NAMATH AND ANN-MARGRET (even if it was just in a movie)
JOE NAMATH AND RANDI OAKES

THE CUTEST OF THEM ALL?
JOE DiMAGGIO AND MARILYN MONROE

Marilyn Barnett, former lesbian lover of Billie Jean King, waits for a ruling on an eviction notice filed by King. (AP/Wide World Photos)

Larry King with his wife Billie Jean King at the press conference where she admitted to having had a homosexual affair. (AP/ Wide World Photos)

Martina Navratilova

Marla Collins autographing her picture in the issue of Playboy for which she was fired from her job as a Chicago Cubs ball girl (Milwaukee Journal)

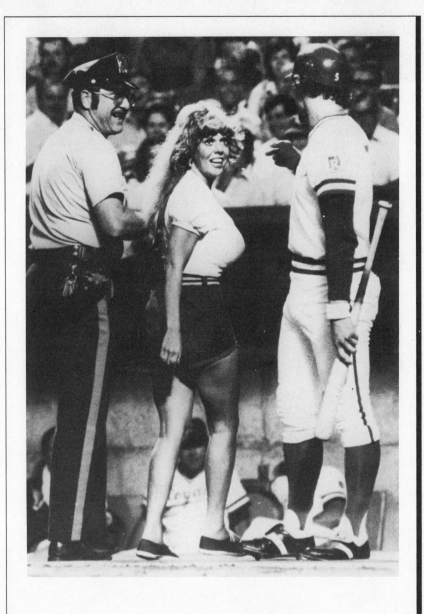

Morganna, the kissing bandit, is arrested in Kansas City after stealing a kiss from George Brett. (AP/Wide World Photos)

George Brett steals a kiss—and a hat and boa—from Morganna during her nightclub show. (AP/Wide World Photos)

Joey Heatherton and Lance Rentzel on their wedding day (AP/ Wide World Photos)

Jan Stephenson chats with Johnny Carson on the "Tonight Show." (AP/Wide World Photos)

Jan Stephenson, dressed in a ti-leaf skirt during a practice round in the 1982 Women's Kemper Open (AP/Wide World Photos)

At sea before the wife swap—New York Yankee pitchers Fritz Peterson and Mike Kekich, with Mrs. Peterson on the left and Mrs. Kekich on the right (AP/Wide World Photos)

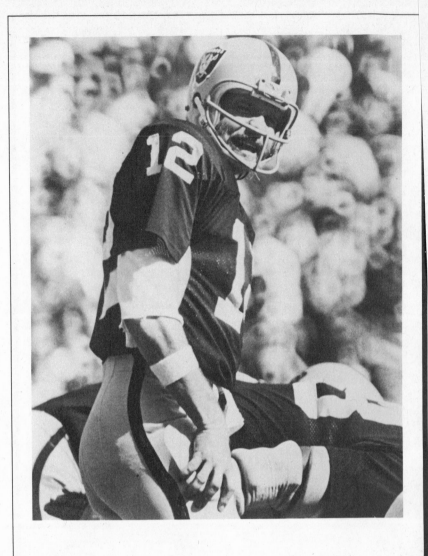

Ken Stabler

Football player Ahmad Rashad and actress Phylicia Ayers-Allen
(AP/Wide World Photos)

Baseball player Ray Knight and golfer Nancy Lopez (AP/Wide World Photos)

Marilyn Monroe and Joe DiMaggio—were they the cutest couple of them all? (AP/Wide World Photos)

TRAGEDIES

MARC BUONICONTI

ROBERTO CLEMENTE

JOE DELANEY

FLO HYMAN

DARRYL STINGLEY

KATHY ORMSBY

RAY MANCINI

THE GIANTS

BOXING WITH AIDS

Young people die and are crippled every day, but a young athlete's death or disablement is met with universal shock. Is it the wasted potential, or is it true love lost to an adoring public?

MARC BUONICONTI

NICK BUONICONTI SR. was a fierce competitor in his own pro football career. While Buoniconti is no longer playing football, he's still competing, but this time the opposition is much tougher than the Pittsburgh Steelers or the Dallas Cowboys; it's spinal paralysis.

Buoniconti suddenly became a full-fledged fighter on October 26, 1985. It was on that day that his son, Marc, severed his spinal cord while playing a college football game for The Citadel.

A linebacker like his father, Marc made an apparently routine tackle of opponent Herman Jacobs, a running back from East Tennessee State. Buoniconti never got up. His limp form on the field was a sign of serious damage; he had severed his spinal cord between two vertebrae and was paralyzed from the neck down. The damage was so severe that he could barely breathe without help from a respirator. "That's when I was really depressed, feeling sorry for myself," said Marc.

Marc's mother and father were not watching the game that day. When they arrived in Johnson City that night, Nick said, "He had tubes in every possible opening. He couldn't talk."

Only days after the accident, Marc was moved to Jackson Memorial Hospital in Miami, where a unique project aimed at wiping out spinal cord paralysis was taking place. One of the doctors involved in the project, Barth Green, approached Nick Sr. for help.

The Miami Project enlisted Nick Sr., the former All-Pro with the Miami Dolphins, to its cause, and they also acquired Nick Jr. as their full-time director of staff development. Marc Buoniconti calls himself the "poster child of paralysis." The Miami Project's goal: to raise $10 million and, with the help of top physicians and scientists in the field, to find a cure for spinal cord paralysis within five years.

Spinal cord paralysis has claimed 500,000 victims in the United States, with 10,000 more joining the ranks each year, most of them young people suffering from motorcycle, football, or diving accidents.

Project officials admit that Marc Buoniconti's accident, while a tragedy, was at the same time a "miracle." With Nick Sr. enlisted, their goal of $10 million went from pipe dream to distinct possibility. Nick Sr. is a highly visible spokesman with an executive position and very powerful friends. He is president of U.S. Tobacco and a commentator on HBO's weekly NFL highlights and news program. His involvement has netted the project millions of dollars. And, as one member of its executive board said, "The Miami Project would exist, but it wouldn't be operational without Marc Buoniconti."

The accident was not without its bitter overtones. The Buonicontis sued The Citadel for unspecified damages, claiming Marc had been playing with an injury of which he was never informed. School officials countered, arguing that Marc was solely responsible because the tackle was illegal—an example of spearing, or hitting the opponent head first.

ROBERTO CLEMENTE

ROBERTO CLEMENTE was hesitant to make the flight on New Year's Eve, 1973. The Pittsburgh Pirates superstar outfielder had organized the effort to aid earthquake-ravaged Nicaragua, and he had chartered the private plane to carry supplies from his home in San Juan, Puerto Rico, to Nicaragua. But at the last minute he hesitated, then said to his wife, Vera, "What the heck. I'll go. Just be sure to have roast pork for me and the kids when I get back."

The plane never made it to Managua. It developed engine trouble on takeoff and attempted to turn back to San Juan, but crashed a mile off shore, in eighty feet of water.

The news stunned not only those in baseball circles but the entire world. Puerto Rican radio stations canceled their regularly scheduled programs and played somber music. Callers flooded the Pittsburgh offices of the wire services, seeking information in the hours after the crash.

What kind of ballplayer could engender such feelings? Clemente was simply one of the best ever to play the game of baseball. His lifetime batting average was .317, precisely the figure he hit for in 1966, when he was named the National League's MVP. He won four batting titles and reached the milestone 3,000-hit plateau on September 30, 1972, only the eleventh player in baseball history to do so at the time. It was to be the last hit of his eighteen-season major-league career.

His unorthodox batting style was "all wrong" according to one baseball expert. But he was credited by *Los Angeles Times* columnist Jim Murray as having one of the greatest single World Series performances ever in 1971, when he hit two home runs, two doubles, a triple, drove in four runs, scored three runs, was robbed of another homer, and finished with a .414 average. Of his fielding, Murray said, "In the outfield, he was the whole book on how to. His arm was bionic."

Described as moody and surly at times, Clemente was also a hypochondriac. But upon his death, friends recalled a side of Clemente few saw. Teammate Willie Stargell, moved to tears, said, "Clemente's work with the relief effort was typical. Roberto was always trying to help someone." Nicaraguan President Anastacio Somoza said in a cable to Clemente's family (including three young sons), "He died a hero, leaving his family in order to aid humanity."

The plane was later termed unsafe to fly, more than two tons overweight, with an engine already damaged from a previous flight, and a crew that included an unqualified flight engineer and copilot who had logged only six hours of flight time in a DC-7. Despite a massive search, no bodies were ever recovered.

Baseball did not forget Clemente in the years that followed. The Baseball Hall of Fame waved its five-year waiting period and inducted Clemente in August 1973.

His widow, Vera, said in 1980, "As time passed, I thought the people of Puerto Rico would always remember Roberto, but I thought the people in the States would probably forget him. But I was wrong, so wrong. It is unbelievable, the extent of love, affection, and respect baseball fans and people in general have for my husband."

JOE DELANEY

THE SCRIPT was all wrong. When football star Joe Delaney jumped into a Louisiana water hole to save three drowning youngsters, the movies would have had him save them all. But they weren't filming a movie on June 29, 1983, when Delaney was drowned attempting to rescue three youngsters in a public park. Two of the three youngsters also died. Harry Holland, Jr., eleven, was pronounced dead just after the incident. Lancer Perkins, also eleven, died several days later.

Delaney, twenty-four, was a star with the Kansas City Chiefs. A handsome young man with a huge smile, he was a first-round draft choice out of Northwestern State. He won a starting position with the Chiefs, gained 1,121 yards his rookie season, was named a starter in the Pro Bowl, and was honored as the AFC rookie of the year. He gained 380 yards in the strike-shortened 1982 season.

Authorities said Delaney, who lived in Ruston with his wife Carolyn and three children, was visiting Monroe for the day. The park had free admission that day to promote a new waterslide, and the three youngsters were swimming in an area authorities said they shouldn't have been in, a hole left by construction workers that was swollen with water from recent heavy rains.

Witnesses said that Delaney yelled to the boys to be careful, but that they slipped into deep water and went under. Hearing the screams for help, Delaney jumped in, despite being unable to swim well himself. Only one of the boys eventually made it to

231

the shore. Delaney and the other two were pulled from the water later by divers.

Teammate Gary Green described Delaney as one of the most well-liked players on the team. "He was just a very happy-go-lucky guy," Green said. "He spent every moment enjoying life. He's . . . a guy that's liked not just for his football antics."

Delaney's heroics did not go unnoticed. The Chiefs' head coach, John Mackovic, said, "I think Joe Delaney was a hero before today. I think people from his high school, his college, and his area could always point to him and say, 'You can be like him.' He was dedicated to his family and dedicated to his sport."

Only weeks after his death, Delaney's wife accepted the nation's highest civilian honor, the Presidential Citizen's Medal, from Vice President George Bush.

FLO HYMAN

SIMPLY AND without argument, Flo Hyman was the best American woman volleyball player ever. Successful, bubbly and fit, she dropped dead on January 24, 1986, during a game in a Japanese all-star league. Doctors in Japan called it a heart attack, but an autopsy performed days later in the United States pointed more correctly to Marfan Syndrome, a mysterious genetic disorder that weakened Hyman's heart, leading to a ruptured aorta, the large artery that carries the entire flow of blood leaving the heart. Sitting on the sideline after leaving for a routine substitution, her aorta literally burst within her chest.

Hyman never knew what hit her. For Marfan Syndrome, which typically haunts tall, lanky people, is nearly impossible to detect— so much so that one expert on the disease said, "Often the first person to make the diagnosis of Marfan's is the coroner."

At 6 feet 5 inches, Hyman was typical of those who have suffered the disease's dread results. She is not the only American sports star to fall victim. Chris Patton, a top basketball player at the University of Maryland, died during a pickup game in 1976, also of Marfan Syndrome.

Hyman's legacy in volleyball did not die with her. At thirty-one she had been part of the United States' rise to prominence in the sport. Growing up in Inglewood, California, and joining the national team in 1975, she suffered through the boycott of the 1980 Olympics. With six teammates, she returned to the 1984 Olympic team that won the silver medal.

A year after Hyman's death, Martina Navratilova donated $150,000 to the Women's Sports Foundation in her name, and on September 22, 1986, Hyman was inducted into the International Women's Sports Hall of Fame.

DARRYL STINGLEY

JACK TATUM put Darryl Stingley in a wheelchair for the rest of his life. After all, it was Jack Tatum who wrote a book entitled *They Call Me Assassin.* It was Jack Tatum who competed with a teammate for "knockouts" and "limpoffs," scoring points for opponents who are carried off or limp off the football field. And Jack Tatum never apologized but instead said, "I could have attempted to intercept, but because of what owners expect of me when they give me my paycheck, I automatically reacted to the situation by going for an intimidating hit. Do I let a receiver have the edge and give him a chance?"

Game reports gave this account of the night of August 12, 1978, when Stingley's New England Patriots were playing Tatum's Oakland Raiders in California: "With one minute twenty-six seconds left in the second quarter, Stingley flew through the air in an attempt to catch a pass in the middle of the field. The ball sailed past him, but Stingley was met by Tatum. For ten minutes Stingley lay motionless as doctors moved him gently to a gurney and wheeled him away."

Stingley hovered near death for days after the accident, suffering from the complications of having his neck broken and becoming a quadriplegic. Later on Stingley admitted that he had even contemplated suicide. But in 1983 he wrote a book of his own, *Happy to Be Alive,* with Mark Mulvoy.

His book described the pain of the therapy and the costs of the injury, to himself and his family.

Exploring his thoughts about the fateful evening, he wrote about the hit itself, "I felt as though I was suspended in mid-air . . . and here was this monster train coming at me full steam. I was looking Tatum dead in the eye and saw his look. His eyes and face were on fire. He was cocking his bone, as we call it, his forearm. And he was coming fast. I saw him (and ducked) but it was too late. I hit the ground with a thud and tried to get up, as I had so many times before, but I couldn't move. . . . I wasn't in pain, or at least I couldn't feel any. I just couldn't move. Not a muscle. Nothing. I couldn't feel my feet. Or my arms. Or my body. I couldn't feel anything. Everything in my body was saying, 'Get up, Darryl,' but I couldn't move."

Stingley said he'll never think the hit was "necessary," and added, "The hit was the essence of Jack Tatum's nature."

Tatum, meanwhile, wrote his own book. And his "no-apology" attitude finally began to affect him. The Raiders quickly dumped Tatum for a bargain-basement price to the Houston Oilers after publication of the book—which was met with severe criticism.

KATHY ORMSBY

KATHY ORMSBY'S potential in track was limitless. Collegiate coaches who saw her perform felt they were witnessing one of the sport's future stars shooting to the top.

That potential was abruptly shattered one night in June of 1986, a night on which it should have continued its upward climb. On that night, Ormsby, a twenty-one-year-old competitor for North Carolina State, ran from the track during the 10,000 meter race in the NCAA championship meet, and jumped off a nearby bridge. The thirty-foot fall to the river bank below left her permanently paralyzed from the waist down.

Labeled a suicide attempt by police, the incident left friends, coaches, and fellow competitors asking one question: Why? Why would an *A* student, an aspiring medical missionary, and an NCAA record holder attempt to end her life?

Six months later, after silence from all involved, Ormsby attempted to answer that question. Ormsby talked about the race. "All of a sudden . . . I just felt like something snapped inside of me. And I was really angry," she said. "I didn't feel like this was me because I didn't usually have reactions like that. That was not a reaction I had as a person, ever."

She ran another lap, though, then left the track. "I couldn't face embarrassment, and not knowing what was happening, again. I just wanted to run away."

She said that she vaguely remembers leaving the stadium, crossing a field, and climbing a seven-foot link fence. "I just ran. And

I just don't feel like that person was me. I know that sounds strange, but I was just out of control. I just couldn't face everybody. I felt like I had let everybody down."

Stories that ran in newspapers and magazines following the tragedy hinted at the pressure young athletes feel in competitive situations. Ormsby's parents, who lived in Rockingham, were labeled anything but pushy. Yet the pressure to perform was apparently there on the night of the race. As one of her teammates put it later, "She's a perfectionist. She's always been a pusher. She'd even bring her notes to our workouts so she could study." Ormsby admitted she had lived by her own strict rules.

Those rules must have been broken the night of the race. For, with two-thirds of the race gone and Ormsby in fourth place, within three strides of the lead, without any hint of what was to come—Ormsby ran off the track, up the stairs, and out of the stadium.

Nearly ten minutes later, a motorist summoned a campus policeman and told him of a problem at a nearby bridge. It was Ormsby, lying below the bridge on the banks of the nearby White River. According to police reports, she told them she had jumped.

A trackside observer, coach Peter Tegen of the University of Wisconsin, recalled what happened. "I thought she was running directly to me. I thought she may have confused me for her coach. I was wearing red and white, the same colors as North Carolina State. It was eerie. Her eyes were focused straight ahead. She didn't look left or right. I thought she was heading for the bathroom—there's a concrete building in that corner with bathrooms in it. That's the last I saw of her. And then she just disappeared beyond the stands."

Ormsby suffered a broken rib, a collapsed lung, and a fractured vertebra, which caused the spinal cord injury that left her paralyzed.

Two days after the incident doctors confirmed that Ormsby would never walk again. She remembers many details from the moment she was found on the ground to the time in the hospital. "The first time you try to get up, that's when it really hits you that it's different," she said.

Was it a planned suicide attempt? Ormsby says no and points to notes she wrote on the day of the race, including a memo to order pizza and maybe dessert after the race. "I think that if I had planned to kill myself, I wouldn't ever have gotten around to it: I would have written so many notes telling people it wasn't their fault," she recalled in a story published in the *Charlotte Observer*.

Later in 1986, Ormsby returned to her parents' home. She learned to drive a car through hand controls and enrolled at a nearby Presbyterian college. Her plans still included the ministry.

RAY MANCINI

FOR A while it seemed everything Ray Mancini touched—that is except his opponents—turned to gold. Born in Youngstown, Ohio, he turned to boxing like a knight after the Grail, seeking to win the world boxing title his father Lenny never got a shot at because of World War II. Ray was even tagged with the same nickname as his dad, "Boom Boom," which described the tenacious style both men employed in the ring.

When he won the World Boxing Association's lightweight title in a first-round knockout over Art Frias in 1982, he seemed to provide the boxing world with everything it needed to gain a bit more notoriety. Mancini was articulate, a devout Catholic, a loyal son, and even more important in the 1980s, he was white. The media flocked to his camp, and his bouts became events, with Sylvester Stallone at ringside for one of them.

But the story turned tragic in November of 1982, when Mancini defended his title against an unheralded South Korean by the name of Duk Koo Kim. Despite his listing as the WBA's No. 1 contender, Kim was not expected to last long against Mancini, but the fighter proved much tougher than his advance billing. Going into the fourteenth round of the scheduled fifteen-round bout, both boxers had taken a beating.

In the fourteenth round, however, Mancini caught Kim with a vicious right that sent the twenty-three-year-old slumping to the canvas.

He never got up.

Carried by stretcher from the ring, Kim was taken to a Las Vegas hospital; after two and a half hours of surgery, doctors said they had removed a blood clot from his head and that the boxer showed no signs of brain function. Mancini, distraught over the events, attended an impromptu mass to pray for his fallen opponent.

Four days later doctors took Kim off a respirator and he was pronounced dead. The surgeon who operated on Kim after the bout said that "in all probability" a small vein was ruptured in the right side of Kim's brain from a single blow thrown late in the fight.

With this death, the antiboxing movement was given a new shot in the arm. But there was little if any criticism of Mancini's tactics or of any officials present at the bout.

Angelo Dundee, one of the sport's top trainers, said, "I don't know of any way it could have been prevented. I know Las Vegas. I know its doctors. I know the promoters, and I know the precautions that are taken. Las Vegas is one of the hotbeds of boxing in the country. They've got shows every night of the week. It couldn't have been prevented."

Mancini postponed his next title defense, and there was talk that he would never fight again. But then, weeks later, he announced he would continue with the sport.

Ironically, only days before Mancini's next bout, Kim's sixty-six-year-old mother was reported to have committed suicide in Korea by drinking poisonous chemicals.

Mancini lost his title in June of 1984 after a fourteen-round knockout at the hands of Livingstone Bramble. The final fight, which ended his boxing career in February of 1985, was also a defeat at the hands of Bramble.

THE GIANTS

WHAT ARE the chances that four young, physically fit men, part of a group of men numbering in only the hundreds, would each come down with cancer? That's what everyone wanted to know after four members of the New York Giants each developed a form of cancer from 1980 through 1987.

One of the four was Dan Lloyd, who discovered in 1980 that he had acute lymphocytic lymphoma. He survived. Karl Nelson was the last of the four. He was diagnosed as suffering from Hodgkin's disease late in 1987 and was scheduled to begin therapy. Two others weren't so lucky. John Tuggle died in 1986 after struggling for two years with angiosarcoma, a rare cancer of the blood vessels. Doug Kotar died of an inoperable brain tumor in 1983, at the age of twenty-nine.

Scientific authorities say that while the odds are against four members of any same team acquiring cancer in a short period of time, it is unlikely that there is any connection.

Despite the authorities, fingers were pointed at the Meadowlands Sports Complex in East Rutherford, New Jersey, where the Giants play. The huge facility was built over landfill and is near a creek in which large deposits of mercury were found.

Claire Gaines, an official of the National Football League Players Association, has asked that tests be performed to see if there was an environmental link to the four cancer cases. The NFLPA, of course, has as its job the representation of the players' interests. And Gaines, who coached at the Meadowlands as a member of the New Jersey Generals (of the now-defunct United States Football League), was discovered to have a benign brain tumor in 1985. "The players are totally and intensely exposed to the elements," Gaines said.

The governing authorities of the Meadowlands Complex, while defending the facility, agreed in 1987 to conduct air, water, and soil tests in the area, but cancer experts have said that because the four cases of cancer were of different types, they saw no likelihood of a common environmental cause. An environmental cause, they say, would likely lead to a single type of cancer. The Associated Press quoted Dr. Frederick Cohen, head of the oncology department at Newark Beth Israel Hospital, as saying, "I'm absolutely convinced there is no connection. Environmental exposure takes many years to induce cancer. These cancers are diverse. It's a matter of coincidence."

BOXING WITH AIDS

BOXERS PROBABLY won't be the only ones with their gloves on in the ring in the near future, thanks to the disease AIDS.

In one hotbed of boxing, New Jersey officials have ordered referees to wear gloves in the ring to protect themselves against the AIDS virus. The state's athletic commissioner, Larry Hazzards, said, "It is common practice for referees to get completely splattered with blood, saliva, and everything else."

No less than Ferdie Pacheco, the NBC television "Fight Doctor," said, according to a quote in *Newsweek,* that while boxers almost never use drugs, the boxing game includes "guys who are casual homosexuals." Others, he said, have spent time in prison, where another high-risk group exists.

Testing boxers for AIDS in the United States may not be far off. Already, foreign boxers entering Britain to fight are being screened on orders of the British Boxing Board. Would it be possible for a boxer to acquire AIDS by being in contact with the blood from another boxer? Boxing officials doubt it, but they don't seem to be taking any chances.

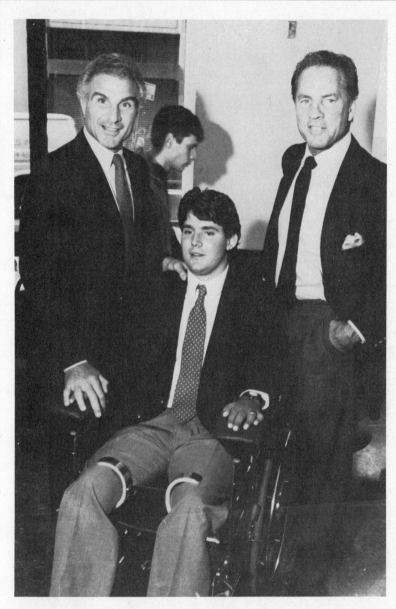

Former Miami Dolphin Nick Buoniconti, left, and son Marc, in a wheelchair, posed with Frank Gifford at a fundraiser. (AP/ Wide World Photos)

Nick Buoniconti in his playing days

Roberto Clemente and his family at a ceremony honoring the star in 1970 (AP/Wide World Photos)

Joe Delaney (AP/Wide World Photos)

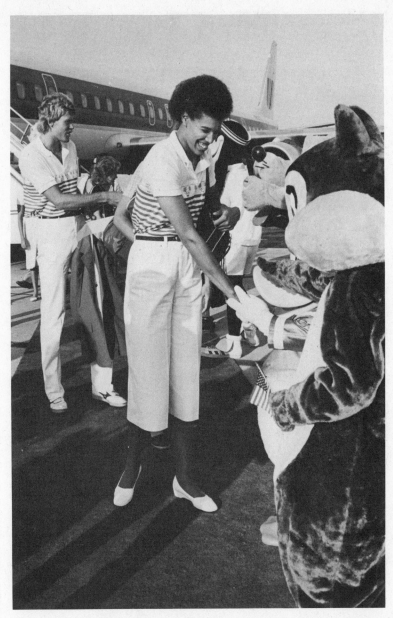

Flo Hyman and a group of American medalists from the 1984 summer Olympics (AP/Wide World Photos)

Jack Tatum delivered the hit that downed Darryl Stingley.

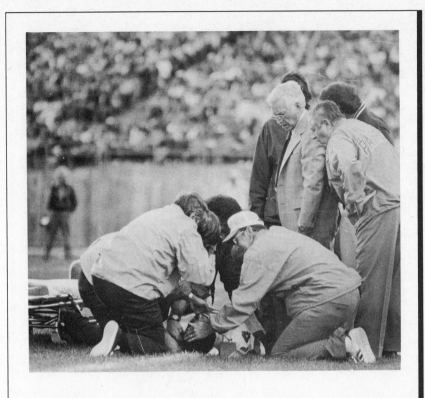

Darryl Stingley lies motionless on the field after his collision with Jack Tatum. (AP/Wide World Photos)

Kathy Ormsby (AP/Wide World Photos)

TROUBLE
WITH
WOMEN

LYMAN BOSTOCK

JIM BROWN

STEVE GARVEY

CLEON JONES

SPIDER SABICH

MARVIN MITCHELSON

WOMAN TALK

DAVE STEWART

Joe Namath managed to shoot down the theory that sex and sports don't mix. Not every athlete can claim to be this lucky and some have found themselves in serious trouble—with women.

LYMAN BOSTOCK

LYMAN BOSTOCK became a millionaire because of baseball. He was a man in the right place at the right time. On the night of September 23, 1978, the twenty-seven-year-old Bostock was in the wrong place, at the wrong time, with the wrong woman, and he died of a shotgun blast to the head.

Bostock was killed while riding in a car with his uncle and two women related to his uncle. Charged with the shooting was Leonard Smith, estranged husband of one of the two women, who said he was following his wife, whom he suspected of having an affair.

Earlier that year Bostock, who broke into the major leagues with the Minnesota Twins, signed a lucrative free-agent contract with the California Angels for $2.7 million over five years. He made more headlines a month into the season when he said he was thinking of donating a month's salary—around $50,000—to charity because of his poor showing at that point, with his batting average at an anemic .147. But Bostock turned himself around during the season and was batting .296 at the time of his death.

Bostock was in Gary, which he called his second home, when the Angels were in nearby Chicago to play the White Sox in a late-season series.

At 10:44 P.M. on Saturday night, a car driven by Smith pulled up to the vehicle in which Bostock was sitting. A shotgun was thrust out the window, and Bostock and twenty-six-year-old Barbara Smith, the apparent target, were hit. Bostock died three hours later.

255

A police spokesman said, "It'll probably come out like he [Bostock] was having some kind of affair with the woman. But it wasn't like that at all. They had been together for a total of about twenty blocks before the shooting. It's just a shame."

Bostock, who was survived by his wife Yuovene, left behind a legacy of admiration. Gene Mauch, Bostock's manager with the Twins, said, "I'm shocked. I'm sorry. I'm angry. I'm sick. People don't realize the strong feelings of admiration and respect that develop on a ball club. I thought the world of that man."

Smith was eventually tried but convinced a jury he was driven to insanity by his wife's infidelity, and was sent to a mental hospital. After only six months he was released when doctors said he was not mentally ill, and a judge ruled that by law he could no longer be held. Indiana homicide law was eventually tightened because of the case. Bostock, however, was dead.

JIM BROWN

WHEN JIM BROWN stepped onto the football field there was little doubt about his reputation. Perhaps the greatest running back in NFL history, Brown left behind a legacy of fame and a list of records. Once off the field, however, his image began to tarnish.

In 1965, at the age of thirty and seemingly at the peak of his game, Brown retired from pro football. He would concentrate, so he said, on a budding acting career and a civil rights organization he had founded.

From Cleveland to Hollywood, Brown never stepped far from the spotlight as his acting career took off. He starred in *Rio Conchos* with Racquel Welch while still in football. Afterwards he played in *The Dirty Dozen, Ice Station Zebra,* and *Riot,* among others.

But another list began to develop: women who accused Brown of assault.

In 1965 he was accused of beating and sexually molesting two teenage girls. One of the teenagers later dropped the charges, and Brown was found innocent of charges filed by the other girl.

In 1968 a twenty-two-year-old model was found lying unconscious under his second-floor balcony when police arrived to investigate a complaint about an argument. The woman failed to press charges.

In 1985 Brown was charged with rape and assault in an incident in which a friend claimed Brown beat and raped her when she refused to engage in sex with him and another woman. Charges

257

were dropped when the District Attorney said he no longer believed in the case because of contradictory allegations and a lack of evidence.

In 1986, at the age of fifty, Brown was arrested for beating his live-in girlfriend, supposedly on the eve of their wedding and her birthday. Debra Clark wound up with a scratch under one eye, a bruised arm, and a possible cracked rib. Several days later, however, she said that she did not want to press charges.

Brown has said little during the years about his conflicts, shrugging them off as easily as tacklers on a field. He explained the last incident, simply saying, "Being who I am, one telephone call creates a thing across the country. As a people event, it was nothing. As a media event, it was something else."

If the exploits had not sullied his Hall of Fame football reputation, Brown took some shots from the media in 1983 when he threatened to return to the game to keep his NFL rushing record of 12,312 yards from falling to either Franco Harris or Walter Payton. "Even if Franco beats my record by 500 yards, I will come back," Brown said. "I think it is better to die with your boots on like an old soldier."

The comeback was short-lived. Payton eventually passed Brown and was past 16,000 yards at the beginning of the 1987 season. Hollywood seemed to give up on Brown, too, for most of the 1980s, until he won a part in a 1987 release, titled, ironically, *The Running Man*.

STEVE GARVEY

IN A sports world often darkened by drugs and dissent Steve Garvey was called "Mr. Clean." The star first baseman for the Los Angeles Dodgers seemed to be perfect. Outstanding on the field, he was the Most Valuable Player in the National League in 1974, and in the All-Star Games in 1974 and 1978. Off the field, he was an honorary chairman of the Multiple Sclerosis Foundation and was named one of the top ten young men in America. His wife, Cyndy, was a beauty and a television personality in Los Angeles. Barbi and Ken, they were called. They seemed to be the perfect couple.

The bubble broke in the summer of 1980, and the pieces fell all over the pages of *Inside Sports,* when Pat Jordan wrote a story called "Trouble in Paradise." The article quoted Cyndy at length and intimated that there was a split in the Garvey household. At one point, Cyndy complained, Steve even missed the birth of a child because of baseball. She also claimed her husband was not showing her affection: "I need to be cuddled, tested, talked to, made love to. . . ."

The national media quickly joined in the story, reprinting excerpts of the tattle-tale story. But Garvey fought back. He filed an $11.2 million lawsuit against *Inside Sports,* charging that the article was "replete with falsehoods, half-truths, and innuendo." Garvey also asked for a restraining order against the *Los Angeles Herald Examiner,* which was about to reprint excerpts. The court ruled that the story could run.

In the suit, the Garveys claimed that even though they were

happily married, the story led readers to believe they were unhappy. They also alleged a breach of contract, saying that the interviews were granted for a "favorable, positively written story about the special challenges of being married to a well-known athlete."

Who should we believe? Baseball fans undoubtedly tried hard to side with the Garveys. But only a year later the Garveys filed for divorce, ending their ten-year marriage. The *Inside Sports* lawsuit was eventually settled out of court.

CLEON JONES

DON'T FALL asleep nude in the back of a van on a city street. That's what happened to Cleon Jones of the New York Mets in the spring of 1975, and it may have helped bring a shining career to an early end.

Jones had been left behind to allow a knee injury to heal when the Mets broke spring training camp for the regular season. But at 5 A.M. on May 4 he was found in the rear of a van in a St. Petersburg parking lane—naked, and asleep with a woman.

Both Jones and the woman, Sharon Ann Sabol, were arrested. Jones was originally charged with disorderly morals, but the charge was changed to indecent exposure before his hearing. Sabol was charged with indecent exposure, possession of marijuana, and possession of narcotics paraphernalia. A little more than a week later, charges against both were dropped.

But that was hardly the end for Jones, who had been a key player in the Mets' 1969 World Series championship. The Mets' chairman of the board, M. Donald Grant, arranged a press conference in which both Jones and his wife were present. Grant said, "Since there is to be no prosecution in Florida, that makes us the judge of what to do with Cleon. We think Cleon is a good man—the type we always have wanted our fans to think we have on our team—but we want him to know he has hurt us, his family, and baseball in general. I told Cleon that he would have to write us an apology."

Jones wrote, "I wish to apologize publicly to my wife and children, the Mets' ownership and management, my teammates, to all Mets' fans, and to baseball in general for my behavior in St. Petersburg May 4. I am ashamed of what I have done, but I can assure you that I have never used drugs or marijuana in any way, shape, or form. I have promised the management that if they permit me to rejoin the team, no one will regret having done so."

Jones's wife said, "I've known Cleon for fifteen years and been married to him for eleven years, and I think he should be given another chance."

If the Mets were hoping this would end the incident they were wrong, but it wasn't Jones who would end up taking the heat.

Marvin Miller, then executive director of the Major League Baseball Players Association, accused the Mets of attempting to humiliate Jones, and added, "The hastily called news conference and the required reading of a prepared 'confession' covering alleged misconduct was deplorable."

Larry Merchant, then a columnist for the *New York Post,* was even more critical of the Mets. He wrote, "Cleon Jones's father fled Mobile, Alabama, because he knew what kind of justice he would get after he beat up a white man who humiliated Mrs. Jones. Would that Cleon Jones had beat up M. Donald Grant at that vile press conference and fled the plantation in Flushing. M. Donald Grant would have got what he deserved. . . ." He added, "M. Donald Grant did that obscene thing. It is he, not Cleon Jones, who owes us an apology. How dare this supercilious blowhard put a man on the rack for the entertainment of presumed moralists in Metland?"

Jones's problems with the Mets weren't over yet. After he refused to enter a game in July, his manager Yogi Berra told the team's management it was he or Jones. Jones was released. He ended up signing on as a free agent with the Chicago White Sox the next spring, but after making the team, he was dropped early in the season.

Out of baseball, he was fined $250 in 1977 after he was arrested in Mobile, and convicted of assaulting two police officers and resisting arrest.

Jones, who finished his career with a .279 batting average, had been stopped for having improper taillights. He claimed he was assaulted by the officers. Jones sustained a head wound, one officer was reported cut, and another suffered a sprained finger.

SPIDER SABICH

ASPEN SEEMED like paradise to Vladimir "Spider" Sabich. A former world professional ski champion, he and his live-in lover Claudine Longet (herself a nationally known figure) could walk down the streets, dine, and drink, all without attracting crowds or setting off a salute of flash bulbs.

The privacy of the former mining town in Colorado was shattered in 1976 when Longet shot Sabich with a handgun. Sabich, thirty-one at the time, bled to death from the wound in his stomach on the way to the hospital.

Longet, a former Las Vegas showgirl and wife of singer Andy Williams, had lived with Sabich for eighteen months in Aspen, where he was a local hero. While their relationship was strained at times, Longet said the two were "in love with each other" the night of March 21, 1976, when she shot Sabich. She swore the shooting was an accident, but was it really?

Police reports showed that Longet had taken one of several guns in the house from a closet and asked Sabich to show her how to use it, claiming she was afraid to be by herself when Sabich went on one of his frequent business trips. Sabich handed her a .22 caliber pistol, saying the safety was on. Longet pointed the gun at Sabich and jokingly said, "Bang, bang." The weapon discharged before she could say "bang" a third time, and Sabich slumped to the floor. Longet said that she called the police and then tried to administer mouth-to-mouth resuscitation.

Authorities charged Longet with reckless manslaughter, a felony that could have put her in prison for ten years and cost her $30,000. During the trial Longet claimed the shooting was purely an accident, but the prosecution hinted at a lover's squabble.

Ironically, the most damning testimony involved Longet's former husband, Williams. The prosecution pointed to a conversation Williams had had after the shooting with Peter Greene, Sabich's next door neighbor, at whose house the Williams children were staying on the night of the shooting.

Prosecutor Ashley Anderson asked Williams, "Would you deny that you told the Greenes that Claudine was a crazy type of gal who liked to drive fast, ski fast, and take chances?"

"I would deny that, yes," Williams answered. "I didn't say that."

Then he added, "I recall thanking them, telling them how grateful I was for their taking care of the children. I may have said, 'I can't believe this thing. It's crazy.' "

Greene's wife was called to the stand, and she testified that Williams had said, "She's a crazy chick. She likes to drive too fast. She likes to ski too fast. She likes to be reckless."

Longet, however, received one break when results of the couple's blood and urine tests were suppressed, along with the contents of her diary. But in the trial audience, rumors circulated about the couple's alleged use of drugs, wild parties, and other affairs.

During early testimony, Longet spoke about her four-year relationship with Sabich, saying, "Spider and I loved each other very much. I think we were the best of friends."

However, under cross-examination she later admitted that by mutual agreement she was looking for another place to live at the time of Sabich's death.

The defense's case rested not only on Longet's testimony but on that of a ballistics expert, who said that he found the safety catch on the black and gray German-made Erma pistol "to be inoperative. The safety bar was put in upside-down."

After testimony ended, with Williams in attendance for support, a jury found Longet guilty of a lesser charge—criminally negligent homicide, a misdemeanor. The lesser offense had a maximum punishment of two years in prison and a $5,000 fine. Prosecutor Anderson, who argued that Longet was negligent in pointing the pistol at Sabich and touching the trigger, said he was happy with the decision.

Before sentencing, Longet requested leniency, telling District

Judge George Lohr that a harsh jail term would adversely affect her three children from her marriage with Williams. "At this point, I don't think there is any more that can be done to me than has been during the last ten months," she pleaded. "My children and I are very close, and I love them very much, and they firmly believe in my innocence. I wonder what they will think when a system they believe in would send me to prison."

Lohr told Longet that while he was convinced that the death was unintentional and that she was a good mother, her conduct "resulted in a death. A crime was committed. No sentence might undermine respect for the law." Noting that Longet had not served any time in jail while awaiting trial, he sentenced her to thirty days in jail and ordered two years of probation.

Longet served her jail term, but it wasn't the end of her case. Aspen residents, some of whom had suggested to reporters the day after the trial ended that Longet should be lynched, gave her the cold shoulder, saying she had brought hordes of reporters to the town and tarnished the area's image as a clean-living but sophisticated community.

Sabich's parents filed a $1.3 million lawsuit against Longet, which was later settled out of court when Longet agreed to pay the couple an unspecified sum.

MARVIN MITCHELSON

Clients of Los Angeles divorce attorney Marvin Mitchelson, who has also helped the wives of Elgin Baylor, Chili Davis, and Lyle Alzado, along with two wives of Jerry Buss, Los Angeles Lakers owner:
- Bertha Hagler, wife of boxer Marvelous Marvin
- Alize Dial, wife of NBA star center Ralph Sampson
- Lisa Strawberry, wife of baseball player Darryl Strawberry
- Linda Allen, wife of Chicago White Sox pitcher Neil Allen

WOMAN TALK

"My ex-wives were all good housekeepers. When they left, they kept the house."

—Ex-featherweight champion boxer
Willie Pep, who has been married five times

"My wife made me a millionaire. I used to have three million."
—Hockey player Bobby Hull after his divorce

"Two years ago I retired from baseball to be closer to my family. Last October, my wife left me."

—Jerry Grote, ex–New York Met

DAVE STEWART

Dave Stewart's outstanding 1987 season with the Oakland As brought him into contention for the Cy Young Award for top pitcher in the America League, and it brought him a heap of praise. That was a far cry from what was heaped on Stewart in January of 1985 when he was still a member of the Texas Rangers.

He was arrested that month in a parked car on a grungy Los Angeles street with a prostitute.

It was later determined that the prostitute, whose name was listed as "Lucille," was a twenty-seven-year-old transvestite.

Stewart ended up being found guilty on soliciting charges, was fined $150, and placed on probation for one year.

Lyman Bostock (AP/Wide World Photos)

Jim Brown in his football days

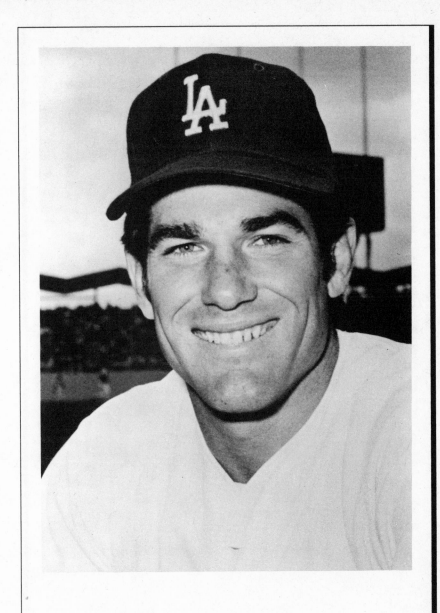

Steve Garvey

Steve Garvey in action

Cleon Jones

Cleon Jones and his wife at a press conference after Jones was cleared of indecent exposure charges (AP/Wide World Photos)

Claudine Longet with her former husband Andy Williams—she was found guilty of negligent homicide in the death of skier Spider Sabich. (AP/Wide World Photos)

Spider Sabich

Marvin Mitchelson with some of his clients (AP/Wide World Photos)